Family and Succession Law in Mexico

Family and Succession Law in Mexico

Second Edition

José Antonio Márquez González

This book was originally published as a monograph in the International Encyclopaedia of Laws/Family and Succession Law.

General Editor: Roger Blanpain
Associate General Editor: Michele Colucci
Volume Editor: Walter Pintens

Wolters Kluwer
Law & Business

Published by:
Kluwer Law International
PO Box 316
2400 AH Alphen aan den Rijn
The Netherlands
Website: www.kluwerlaw.com

Sold and distributed in North, Central and South America by:
Aspen Publishers, Inc.
7201 McKinney Circle
Frederick, MD 21704
United States of America
Email: customer.service@aspenpublishers.com

Sold and distributed in all other countries by:
Turpin Distribution Services Ltd.
Stratton Business Park
Pegasus Drive, Biggleswade
Bedfordshire SG18 8TQ
United Kingdom
Email: kluwerlaw@turpin-distribution.com

ISBN 978-90-411-5886-4

This title is available on www.kluwerlawonline.com

The Author

Dr José Antonio Márquez González graduated from the Faculty of Law of the University of Veracruz with honours. He specialized in Private law and obtained the degree of Doctor in Law at the National University of Mexico. Later on, he took postgraduate courses in civil and international commercial law in Spain, Italy, Austria, Brazil and the US.

Dr Márquez González has published several books and essays in specialized magazines both Notaries' official magazines in Mexico and abroad. He was the director of 'Escribano', and 'Revista Notarial', and he is member of the editorial counselling of 'Estudios Jurídicos' and 'Lawyers of Veracruz' reviews.

He has participated in TV programmes on scientific disclosures with the National University and belongs to the Association of Professors of the Mexican Notary Law Academy. He is also a lecturer, visiting professor at various universities in the country, and National Researcher.

Dr Márquez González is currently a corresponding member of several associations and academies. He also belongs to the Mexican Notaries' International Affairs Committee and the International Informatic Commission. He was also President of the American Notarial Academy and since 2010 a Mexican counsellor before the International Association of Notaries.

At present, Dr Márquez González works as a notary public in Orizaba and has been teaching Civil Law and Family Law at the University of Veracruz for twenty-eight years.

The Author

Table of Contents

The Author 3

List of Abbreviations 11

Preface 13

General Introduction 15

§1. General Background of the Country (Demographic Data) 15

§2. Historical Background of Family and Succession Law 15

§3. Sources of Family and Succession Law 16
I. Constitution 16
II. Legislation 16
III. Treaties 17
IV. Jurisprudence 18

§4. The Courts Administering Family and Succession Law 18

Part I. Persons 21

Chapter 1. The Status of a Person 21

§1. Definition of a Person 21

§2. Capacity 22

§3. Absentees 23

Chapter 2. Registration of Civil Status 25

§1. The Registrar 25

§2. Registers and Certificates 25

I. Birth Certificates 26
II. Certificates of Recognition 27
III. Certificates of Adoption 27
IV. Certificates of Guardianship 28
V. Certificates of Emancipation 28
VI. Marriage Certificates 28
VII. Divorce Certificates 29
VIII. Death Certificates 29
IX. Certificates of Inscription of Statements that Declare or Modify the Marital Status 29
X. Certificates of Correction, Modification and Clearing Up of the Own Certificates of the Registry 29

Chapter 3. Personal Rights 31

Chapter 4. Names 33

§1. Composition of a Name (First Name, Surname, Individual Name, Title of Nobility) 33

§2. Surname 34
I. Acquisition of the Surname 34
II. Change of the Surname 35

§3. First Name 36

Chapter 5. Nationality 38

Chapter 6. Domicile and Residence 40

Chapter 7. Mentally Handicapped Persons 42

Part II. Family Law 45

Chapter 1. Marriage 45

§1. The Nature of Marriage 45

§2. The Capacity to Marry 46

§3. Formalities of Marriage 47

§4. Effects of Marriage 49

§5. Void and Voidable Marriages 52

Chapter 2. Divorce 55

§1. Grounds 55

§2. Procedure 55

§3. Effects 60

Chapter 3. Cohabitation without Marriage 62

Chapter 4. Filiation 64

§1. Children Born in Wedlock 64

§2. Children Born Out of Wedlock 66

Chapter 5. Adoption 71

Chapter 6. Parental Authority 76

Chapter 7. Guardianship 81

Chapter 8. Kinship and Relationships of Affinity 89

Part III. Matrimonial Property Law 91

Chapter 1. Rights and Obligations of Spouses 91

§1. General Principles 91

§2. The Household Expenses 92

§3. The Matrimonial Home 92

§4. Transactions between Spouses 93

Chapter 2. The Marriage Settlement 95

Chapter 3. Conventional Matrimonial Regimes 96

Chapter 4. The Legal Matrimonial Regime 100

Part IV. Succession Law 101

Chapter 1. Intestate Succession 101

§1. The Opening of the Succession 101
I. Death 101
II. Missing Persons and Absentees 102

§2. The Heir 103
I. Capacity to Succeed 103
II. Simultaneous Death 103
III. Unworthiness to Succeed 103

§3. Succession Rules 106
I. The Classes of Heirs 106
A. Surviving Spouse 107
B. Descendants 107
C. Ascendants 108
D. Collaterals 108
E. Concubines 108
II. Representation 109
III. Adoption 109

§4. The Rights of State on the *Bona Vacantia* 110

Chapter 2. Testamentary Succession 111

§1. The Capacity to Make a Will 111

§2. Different Types of Wills 113

§3. The Joint Will 120

§4. Revocation of a Will 120

§5. Provisions in a Will 121

§6. Restrictions 122
I. The Legitim 123
II. Maintenance Provisions 123

§7. Interpretation of a Will 124

Chapter 3. Acts *Inter Vivos* Related to the Estate 126

§1. Estate Planning 126

§2. Donations 127

§3. Trusts 127

§4. Insurance Contracts 129

§5. Others 131

Chapter 4. Acquisition and Administration of the Estate 133

§1. The Acquisition of the Estate 133

§2. The Administration of the Estate 137

Selected Bibliography 145

Index 149

List of Abbreviations

CCBC	Civil Code of Baja California
CCBCS	Civil Code of Baja California Sur
CCCDF	Código Civil Comentado del Distrito Federal (Institute for Legal Research, National University of Mexico)
CCDF	Civil Code of the Federal District
CCESP	Civil Code of Spain
CCGRO	Civil Code of Guerrero
CCGTO	Civil Code of Guanajuato
CCJAL	Civil Code of Jalisco
CCMEX	Civil Code of the State of Mexico
CCMICH	Civil Code of Michoacan
CCMOR	Civil Code of Morelos
CCNAY	Civil Code of Nayarit
CCOAX	Civil Code of Oaxaca
CCPUE	Civil Code of Puebla
CCQROO	Civil Code of Quintana Roo
CCSON	Civil Code of Sonora
CCTAB	Civil Code of Tabasco
CCTAMPS	Civil Code of Tamaulipas
CCTLAX	Civil Code of Tlaxcala
CCVER	Civil Code of Veracruz
CCYUC	Civil Code of Yucatan
CCZAC	Civil Code of Zacatecas
CIC	Citizen's Identity Document
CPCDF	Civil Procedures Code of the Federal District
CPCVER	Civil Procedures Code of Veracruz
CPEUM	Political Constitution of the Mexican United States
CPEV	Political Constitution of Veracruz
CCo	Code of Commerce

List of Abbreviations

CURP	Population Registry's Unique Key
DJM	Diccionario Jurídico Mexicano (Institute for Legal Research, National University of Mexico)
EJ	Estudios Jurídicos (Institute for Legal Research, University of Veracruz)
FCHGO	Family Code of Hidalgo
FCMICH	Family Code of Michoacan
FCMOR	Family Code of Morelos
FCSIN	Family Code of Sinaloa
FCSON	Family Code of Sonora
FCYUC	Family Code of Yucatan
FCZAC	Family Code of Zacatecas
LARCP	Law of Religious Associations and Public Cult
LCS	Law concerning Insurance Contract
LFBC	Family Law of Baja California
LGP	General Population Law
LGTOC	General Law of Securities and Credit Operations
LIAPDF	Institutions of Private Assistance Law of the Federal District
LIE	Foreign Investment Law
LNCM	Navigation and Maritime Trade Law
LN	Nationality Law
LOTSJDF	Organic Law of the Superior Court of Justice of the Federal District
LPFHGO	Family Law of Hidalgo
LSS	Social Insurance Law
RDC	Revista de Derecho Civil (Government of the Federal District)
RDN	Revista de Derecho Notarial (National College of Mexican Notaries)
RDP	Revista de Derecho Privado (Institute for Legal Research, National University of Mexico)
RFDM	Revista de la Facultad de Derecho de Mexico (National University of Mexico)
RMD	Revista Mexicana de Derecho (College of Notaries of the Federal District)
RMJ	Revista Mexicana de Justicia (Government of the Federal District)
RRCDF	Civil Registry Regulations of the Federal District
SCJN	Supreme Court of Justice
SJF	Semanario Judicial de la Federación

Preface

The Mexican United States form a wide territory which stretches from the Gulf of Mexico to the Pacific Ocean, and from the deserts of far North to the humid jungles in the South East, with a population of more than 118 million of inhabitants, and joined in a complex racial and cultural mosaic that gives a great level of heterogeneity to all of its institutions.

Moreover, for many years the country has been involved in a deep process of transformation of its institutions. The opening of the country to foreign trade and the internal democratization process, nowadays, are part of national life. Obviously, the juridical aspect could not escape this slow but consistent institutional transformation.

The review that follows intends to show in a brief and panoramic way, the main institutions of family and succession law in our country. It has been attempted to refer to the characteristics of these juridical branches mainly to the Civil Code in force in Mexico City. Such legislation has been used, in most cases, as a model for other provincial codes, but also the fact that Mexico City continues to centralize the dynamics of national life is taken into great consideration.

Nevertheless, it has been considered important to mention concrete cases of exception, with constant references to local civil codes in the states. Besides, each of the institutions has been analysed, trying to reach an adequate balance between the information of the different codes, the juridical national doctrine and the important sentences of the federal tribunals.

In this way, the reader will be able to understand properly, up to where possible in a review of this magnitude, the current state of family and succession laws in Mexico.

General Introduction

§1. General Background of the Country (Demographic Data)

1. The Mexican United States consists of a total of thirty-two federal entities, including the federal district. Each one of them takes, for its internal regime, as set forth in Article 115 of the Political Constitution of the Mexican United States (CPEUM, 1917), the republican form of government and with full autonomy within its territorial boundary. In the Constitution, Articles 42–48 establish the geographic areas that constitute the national territory, the integrating parts of the Federation and the erection of Mexico City in a federal district as headquarters of the Union and capital of the country.

The Republic's territory consists of a total of nearly 2 million km^2. The most populated cities are Mexico City (20.4 million), Guadalajara (4.4 million), Monterrey (3.7 million), Puebla (2.7 million), Toluca (2.1 million), Tijuana (1.4 million), Leon (1.4 million) and Juarez (1.3 million). All data was estimated to the year 2010, when the last census was done, except the data concerning Mexico City (2013).

§2. Historical Background of Family and Succession Law

2. The Mexican Republic follows the juridical tradition of the Romanist system, which has its origin in the Justinianean compilation of the sixth century A.D., in Bizancio and then passed on to the Medieval Age in a complex mixture with local laws (as the *droit de costume* in France and the Spanish local powers –*fueros*). Later on, this amalgam of laws would reach its ending in compilations that would be more extensive each time, such as the *Siete Partidas* and the *Recopilación de Leyes de los Reinos de las Indias*.

3. Nevertheless, even the colonial law born in Mexico in the sixteenth century would collide with indigenous local customs coming from a tradition and even from an ideological scheme which is completely different to that which is possible and widely found even today. With the arrival of the Hispanic colonies' independence, the process started to grow even more in complexity due to the necessity to provide the newly born republics legal recognition, adapting in this way the European advances of the age. Thus, early on Mexican Republic new civil codes started to be drawn up, outstanding among them, the ones from Oaxaca and Zacatecas because of their being the first; and the civil codes of the Federal District of 1870 and 1884, including important laws on religion, marriage, civil registry and family in general, stated in the Reformation Laws proclaimed by President Benito Juarez in 1856 and 1859.

It is important to clarify here that the civil codifications have a profound influence from the *Code Napoleon* of 1804 and the Austrian, Dutch and Cerdeña civil projects, and even from the Spanish project from Florencio García Goyena.[1]

4. Some time later, the first years of the twentieth century were convulsive times due to the revolution started in 1910, but even in these conditions it would provoke the outburst of important laws in family matters, such as the Divorce Law of 1914 and the Law of Family Relations of 1917, both drawn up by Venustiano Carranza.

The Civil Code of the Federal District (CCDF) that is currently into force was promulgated in 1928, but it did not come into force until 1932.[2]

§3. Sources of Family and Succession Law

5. As was mentioned in the first paragraph, our country maintains a federal-type political structure with entities that result in their autonomous administration and in the expedition of the laws whose competence is not drawn from the federal area, in terms of Articles 117 and 124 of the CPEUM, the last of which establishes that those faculties that are not expressly granted by the Constitution to the federal government, must be understood as being reserved for the states.

I. Constitution

6. In spite of the aforesaid, the dogmatic part of the Constitution establishes some requirements in family law that results in obligatory observance in the local civil codes. Thus, it is stated in Article 4 CPEUM that males and females are equal before the law. That law protects the organization and development of the family; it says that every person has the right to decide in a free, responsible, and informed way about the number and the timing of his children, and that every family has the right to enjoy a dignified and decent housing. Likewise, it is the parents' duty to preserve the right of children to mental and physical health, watching the principle of 'superior interest of the minor'.

However, Article 16 CPEUM complements this disposition stating that 'Nobody can be bothered in his person, family, residence, papers or possessions, but in view of written statement from the competent authority, that settles and motives the legal cause of the procedure'.

II. Legislation

7. According to the Mexican judicial system, the federal authorities do not have the faculties to legislate in civil law matters in what corresponds to family and

1. F. García G., *Concordancias, motivos y comentarios del Código Civil Español* (Mexico, s/e, 1881).
2. As has been mentioned, this Code has brought very important reforms since June 2000, May 2010, and April 2013.

succession law, in the terms stated in the Article 124 CPEUM, from a reserved competence to the local entities.

Therefore, it is at a local level – that means, in each one of the thirty-one federal entities plus the Federal District – where these matters are regulated, precisely in the general civil codes corresponding to every one of the federative entities.

The civil codes can offer a great variety in their dispositions and even in their structure, but it is possible to discern a certain uniformity in all of them, especially if we take the CCDF as a model.

Generally, the local codes have taken this Code as a starting point and therefore this legislation will be used as a model, with the peculiarities that might be found in other civil codes, especially in those that have been drawn up at a more recent date.[3]

8. However, it is also necessary to finally take into account that some states have dictated specific dispositions over family law. These laws are: Family Code of Zacatecas (1986, with many reforms in 2007), Family Code of Morelos (2006, with many reforms in 2007–2008), Family Law of Hidalgo (2007), Family Code of Michoacan (2008), Family Law of Baja California (2011), Family Code of Sonora (2011), Family Code of Yucatan (2012), and Family Code of Sinaloa (2013).

III. Treaties

9. Along with these norms which are found in the highest legislative hierarchy, the Constitution also foresees that all international treaties that are found according to it, with the Senate's approval, will thus constitute the supreme law of the Union (Article 133 CPEUM). Thus, the local judges in every federative entity will adhere to such Constitution, federal laws and treaties, in spite of the opposing dispositions that might exist in local laws.

Our country has signed different international treaties, subscribed by the President of the Republic and approved by the Senate, among which it is necessary to mention the Inter-American Convention on Alimony and Child Support Obligations and the Inter-American Convention on International Minors Restitution, both signed in Montevideo on 15 July 1989.

3. From this point of view, it is necessary to indicate the expedition dates of the local codes to see the temporary rate in which those are situated. Thus, the states that have the oldest civil codes are Federal District (1932), Veracruz (1932), Nuevo Leon (1935), Chiapas (1938), Hidalgo (1940), Sinaloa (1940), Campeche (1943), Oaxaca (1944), San Luis Potosi (1947), Aguascalientes (1948), Durango (1948), Sonora (1949), Colima (1954), Guanajuato (1967), Baja California (1974), Chihuahua (1974), and Tlaxcala (1976).

In the last three decades, the ones from Quintana Roo (1980), Nayarit (1981), Puebla (1985), Zacatecas (1986), Tamaulipas (1987), Queretaro (1990), Guerrero (1993), Morelos (1994), Yucatan (1994), Jalisco (1995), Tabasco (1997), Baja California Sur (1997), Coahuila (1999), State of Mexico (2002), and Michoacan (2008) have been drawn up.

10. In the matter of succession law, the Convention that establishes the Uniform Law over the Form of an International Will, signed in Washington on 26 October 1973 still applies.

IV. Jurisprudence

11. Since our country has absorbed the Romanist system, the primary source of law is the legal text, with the hierarchy that was left exemplified in the previous numerals. However, in some cases, custom and jurisprudence can become formal sources of law as well. Their importance, nevertheless, is far minor: as for custom, it is expressly established that no other custom or practice on the contrary can be discussed against the observance of the law and, even more, it is reassured that the principle of civil judgments must be solved precisely according to the rule of law and its juridical interpretation, where the tribunals play an important role through the interpretation of the norm in the sentences pronounced by them.

12. However, even in this case, the interpretations dictated by the tribunals must fulfil certain requirements, without which its application does not have legal strength.

These requirements consist of five resolutions or sentences dictated precisely in the same sense; the cases must be similar and must not have been interrupted by a decision in the opposite sense. When such requirements have been fulfilled, it is said that tribunals have settled *jurisprudencia* over some specific case.

§4. The Courts Administering Family and Succession Law

13. Following from what was previously said, it must be stated that, generally, the tribunals that administer justice in cases of family and succession law are the same tribunals that are in charge of solving all kinds of civil cases (properties, successions, contracts). For instance, justice, in each one of the federative states, is administered by courts of first instance that solve cases of civil matters and mercantile law at the same time. They are presided over by a single judge, a secretary and an actuary, plus the administrative personnel necessary in their various functions.

As for Mexico City, there are judges specialized in family law, besides judges in civil matters in general, according to Article 2 of the Organic Law of the Superior Court of Justice of the Federal District (*Ley Orgánica del Tribunal Superior de Justicia del Distrito Federal*, LOTSJDF, 1996). These judges of family matters are aware of all voluntary jurisdictions related to family law, as well as the judgments that refer to marriage, its illicitness or voidness; divorce, modifications or rectifications of the Civil Registry's acts, parenthood, food, paternity and filiation, parental authority, interdiction, guardianship, absence and death presumption and family patrimony. They are also concerned with affairs related to succession judgments (Article 52 LOTSJDF).

In Veracruz, Article 117 of the Civil Procedures Code of Veracruz (CPCVER) states: 'Of the matters inherent to the family, will be all acquainted by the judges of the first instance of family matters', according to the legal amendment from 1992. However, at the time of revision of this monograph, in practice the creation of these courts has not taken place yet.

The second instance at this local level is constituted by the superior tribunals of justice, compounded by halls (*salas*) and integrated in each one of them by magistrates. The halls of family matters know of all kinds of matters against resolutions dictated by judges on this matter in the Federal District, as well as of the civil responsibility that may arise.

Finally, the minor quantity is delegated to municipal courts – that also receive the denomination of Courts of Peace. As for the Federal District, Courts of Peace have competence up to the amount of MXN 64,760, that results in 1,000 times the minimum daily salary in force in the Federal District (USD 4,900 approximately, to February 2014).

Part I. Persons

Chapter 1. The Status of a Person

§1. Definition of a Person

14. The CCDF does not define in any of its articles the concept of a person. Diversely, some other civil codes in the Republic do contain a definition, as in the case of the CC of Veracruz, which states in Article 24: 'To the effects of civil law, person is that being or entity holder of rights and obligations' and it is the same case as the Civil Code of Michoacan, that states 'Human people are physical persons' according to a recent reform of Article 16 (December 2010). Similarly, Article 59 of the Civil Code of Morelos mentions that 'Individual legal person is every human being from conception to natural death, having rights and obligations'.

In any case, the civil codes make clear that legal capacity of the people is acquired by birth and lost by death. Nevertheless, the codes recognize expressly the doctrine of the *nasciturus*, stating that ever since the moment that an individual is conceived, the law grants its protection, and legally the presumption is established that 'it has been already born' to the law.

15. As it is known, the law distinguishes between *physical* persons and *moral* persons. The first ones receive also the denomination of *natural persons*, as in Quintana Roo and Guerrero, or *individual juridical persons*, as in Sonora and Morelos. The second ones also receive the denomination, more simple, of *juridical persons*, as in Puebla, Quintana Roo, Guerrero, Jalisco, Baja California Sur, and Tlaxcala. The denomination of *collective juridical persons* is a concept much more correct, as in Sonora, Morelos, and Tabasco.

More than a simple definition, the law displays a list of all of those entities that are recognized as moral persons. Thus, Article 25 of the CCDF mentions the Nation, the Federal District, the states and the municipalities; the other corporations of public character, the civil or commercial societies; the unions; the cooperative and mutual societies; the associations that propose political, scientific, artistic, professional, and recreational goals, and the foreign societies.

An important reform took place referring to the regulation of records of religious people under the legal reform of 'religious association' (AR) which has already been previewed in the Law of Religious Associations and Public Cult (*Ley de Asociaciones Religiosas y Culto Público*, LARCP) issued by former president Carlos Salinas de Gortari, 1992. Since then, in the period of twenty-two years, they have registered almost 8,000 religious associations covering a very long range of religions.[4]

§2. Capacity

16. We have already stated that, with respect to physical persons, the capacity by general rule is acquired by birth, apart from the case of the *nasciturus* that has been already mentioned before. At this point the Mexican civil doctrine distinguishes, in a very clear form, the capacity of enjoyment from the capacity of exercise, understanding by the first the right to enjoy all rights and prerogatives that the law grants; in exchange, in view of the second, the subject disposes of this capacity of exercise precisely in order to make the conceded rights worth.

The capacity to exercise these rights is acquired at eighteen years of age, according to Article 646 CCDF and that is the same limit in all of the other civil codes of the Mexican Republic, following the rule foreseen in the Article 34 CPEUM that states that 'Citizens of the Mexican Republic are all of those men and women that, having the quality of Mexicans, fulfill in addition –the following requirements: I. Having become eighteen years-old; and II. Having achieved an honest way of living.'[5]

17. As far as moral persons are concerned, the law establishes that, once legally constituted, these can exercise all of the rights that are necessary for the accomplishment of the acts that constitute the object of its institution (Article 26). In the case of these moral persons, such capacity is exercised by its representation, either

---

4. Former President Felipe Calderón proposes in 2007 the programme 'October, the civil associations month', whereas civil society organizations, notaries public, and federal and state authorities have coordinated their efforts to obtain very low rates, exemption in certain procedures and taxes and a single point of contact for processing to all the civil associations and societies dedicated to altruistic activities, of communitarian organization or social development, education, health, ecology, culture, human rights, science and technology, etc. Its reason derivates from the fact that more than 50% of civil organizations in the whole country lack of a legal registration, which restricts their access to resources of federal founds and, moreover, provokes problems of illegal representation, manipulation of decisions, deviations towards political goals, illicit enrichments, and so forth.

   For instance, to form a society during October, notaries charge the amount of USD 300; this means, about 40% its normal value during the rest of the year. It happens the same way with societies' regularizations or modifications, shareholders' entry and leaving, and changes in board of directors.

   Due to the success that the programme had, President Calderón, in agreement with governmental offices, extended the programme duration to the whole year, so that now there is no time limit.
5. The Art. 2 of CCDF states that the legal capacity is the same for both sexes and that nobody by a reason of age, sex, pregnancy, marital status, race, language, religion, ideology, sexual orientation, genre identity or expression of role of genre, color, national origin or position social, work or profession, economic status, physical disability or health condition, can be discriminated in services, benefits or rights (2008).

   According to this law, the Art. 23 refers that the legal incapacities are just *restrictions to the capacity*, but they are not in anyway *restrictions to the personality*, as mentioned in the Art. 23 now repealed (cfr. Art. 22, CCMICH and Art. 22 CCHGO). It occurs in the opposite way that in the State of Mexico and Queretaro state, where the laws, even reformed in 2002 and 2010, are still stating that they are 'restrictions to the *personality*' (Art. 2.2 CCMEX and 23 CCQRO).

by virtue of legally expressed disposition, or by virtue of that specifically stated in the corporate charter.

18. In a directly opposite sense, the capacity of persons involves the study that refers to the specific suppositions of *incapacity*. Causes of incapacity are constituted in a physical person, underaging[6] and even in the majority, in the cases of mental disturbance or affection originated by disease or persistent deficiency of a physical character, psychological or sensorial or because of the addiction to toxic substances, such as alcohol, psychotropics or narcotics. This limitation or mental alteration must cause, in a direct form, incapacity to govern or function, or also the incapacity to express their own will by any other means.[7]

19. In concordance with the most accepted doctrine, these incapacities are divided into natural and legal and, precisely, it is specified in Article 450 CCDF. As a matter of fact, our legislation recognizes expressly the phenomenon known as 'state of interdiction', that literally picks up the old Latin expression *interdictio-onis* which means 'that who was forbidden or can't talk for himself'. As it is obvious, the executed acts by interdict people are void.

§3. Absentees

20. A special case is constituted by the people who become related to *absent* or *ignored* persons. The CCDF establishes expressly the provision with respect to the person who might have been absent from the place of his residence, ignoring the place where he is and ignoring if he left a representative of his business as well. In this case, the judge must name a trustee of the goods that might eventually appear in the name of this absent person and must proceed to appoint him by means of edicts published in the main newspapers from the last known domicile.

Past a term that fluctuates between three and six months and if the person does not show up, a judge will proceed then to name a representative. This representative could be, in the terms established in Article 653, the absentee's own spouse, one of his children, the closest ascendant in degree, or even the assumed heir.

In the terms set out in Article 650, this representative becomes the legitimate administrator of the absentee's assets, but with the obligations, faculties and restrictions that tutors have, receiving a retribution that in no case will be less than 5% or more than 10% of taxable income of such assets. The same incapacities, excuses, and restrictions, that are applied to the charge of tutor are applied to this representative, too.

---

6. At this precise point it should be said that a large number of civil codes of the Republic contain specific sections referring to childhood and under-aged. This is the case of the civil codes of Guerrero, Jalisco, Quintana Roo, Tabasco, Tlaxcala, and the Family Code of Sinaloa. However, Zacatecas and Veracruz account with particular laws, that is to say, Children's Rights Law (*Ley de los Derechos del Niño*) and Law of Social Assistance and Protection of Boys and Girls (*Ley de Asistencia Social y Protección de Niños y Niñas*), respectively.
7. The CCHGO includes in its Art. 271 fraction V those blind from birth.

When two years have passed counted from the date when the representative was named, the action to legally request the declaration of absence begins to take place. This action can be exercised, in the terms set out in Article 673, by the legitimate assumed heirs, by the heirs that might be in his or her will, by the persons who maintain some right or obligation that might depend on the life, death or presence of the absentee, and even by the Public Ministry.

Following, the judge announces the request with the necessary publications and after four month's time from the last publication, the judge legally declares the absence for the corresponding legal effects. It might happen that once legally declared absent, the absentee shows up, in which case he must recover his assets, except the yieldings, that must be given to those who had provisional possession.

21. After six years have passed since the declaration of absence, the declaration of assumed death can be requested from the judge. However, there are exceptional cases that might abbreviate this long term, when it concerns accidents, in which case only two years are demanded and these terms can even be decreased to only six months if there is a founded assumption that the missing person was found at the place of the accident or catastrophe.[8]

8. It has already been mentioned that in the CCDF it is required to pass the two-year time period – starting since the naming of the representative – to request the declaration of absence. As for the CC of the State of Guerrero, it does not mention any period of time (Art. 250) to declare the absence, which conforms a strange singularity.

Terms vary again when it is about the assumption of death, because if the CCDF demands six years in the ordinary cases, the codes from Jalisco and Coahuila demand only three years, and the one in Guerrero only two years time.

In case of war, sinester, disaster, and kidnapping, the legal term can be reduced to just three months, and without the in other way necessary declaration of absence (Art. 4.373 CCMEX).

Chapter 2. Registration of Civil Status

§1. The Registrar

22. In every federative entity and in Mexico City there is a registration of civil acts, marital, and family status of people as well. This registration is found in the charge of functionaries who, as for Mexico City, have the name of judges of the Civil Registry. In other cases, however, they are called registrars, in charge officials, officials of the Civil Registry and even judges of peace.[9]

These judges of the Civil Registry are found under the coordination of the titular of the registry, who has the character of Central Judge of the Civil Registry in the Federal District. In order to become a judge, a series of requirements must be fulfilled, among which are, naturally, to be a Mexican by birth, to have a registered title of law, a minimal professional practice of four years, not to be a minister of any religious cult, not to have been condemned for an intentional crime and to pass an admission exam as stated in Article 13 of the Civil Registry Regulations of the Federal District (*Reglamento del Registro Civil del Distrito Federal*, RRCDF). The faculties that these judges have are found in Article 16 of the RRCDF and they are to authorize the acts of the marital status; to draw certified copies of the acts – that must not exceed three working days –; to maintain the updating of the index and catalogues, and others related acts.

By the way, a 2011 reform of the General Population Law (*Ley General de Población*, LGP, 1974), Articles 47–62, refers to the computerized identification of the eye's iris image in order to make the registration in the so-named National Register of Citizens.

§2. Registers and Certificates

23. All facts concerning the civil status of persons must be registered, such as births, child recognition, adoption, marriage, divorce, death, inscription of statements about absence, assumption of death, tutoring, and incapacity in general (Article 35 CCDF).[10]

The registration is public, as anyone can ask for a testimony of the related acts, paying the corresponding fees for the expedition service.

All acts relating to the civil registration of people must be recorded in special formats for each of the susceptible acts to be registered. These acts are called 'forms of the civil registry' and are drawn up in triple form. There is a numerical control of these forms, because they can only be drawn by the executive authority in the

9. The denomination of *Civil Registry* is almost unanimous in all of the codes of the Mexican Republic, with the remarkable exception of the state of Hidalgo, where it shows the denomination of Family State's Registration (*Registro del Estado Familiar*) (Art. 402 FCHGO).

10. This Article has been first reformed in 2004, and then in 2008. The last reform included a new sort of record – the one of gender reassignment. It is a birth certificate to recognize the genre identity, this means, the personal non-volunteer condition of belonging to the masculine genre or to the feminine, and that may be different to the original sex. In this case, it is necessary a special trial. The procedure is stated in Arts 95, 255 and 498, CPCDF.

Federal District or in the federative entities. It is expressly established that the registration of the status of people is proven exclusively within these kinds of certificates, except in isolated cases when there have been no registrations or these have been lost or destroyed, in which case the proof will be replaced with some other document or by witness information (Articles 39–40).

Besides, every one of the forms of the Civil Registry, which are numbered and have the official seal of the entity, carry a number that corresponds to the Population Registry's Unique Key (*Clave Única del Registro de Población*, CURP), according to Article 91 of LGP. In Mexico City the Civil Registry forms can be drawn up in *Braille* language, and in other four indigenous languages (Article 36 CCDF, 2012).

As it was mentioned before, there is a special format for every act. Thus, there are birth certificates, child recognition, adoption, guardianship, emancipation, marriage, divorce, burial, inscription of statements that declare or modify the marital status and, finally, rectification, modification and clarifying of all such acts.[11]

Ensuring the authenticity of the Civil Registry records in these formats, the testimony or certified copy of the registrations may be used as proof for trials.

Serious penalties are established for any falsification, alteration or destruction of registrations (Article 46). As for how much it does to the document itself, the penalty is voidness, except in the case of the civil codes of Sonora (Article 132) and Veracruz (Article 656), that declare the corresponding act as radically 'non-existent'.[12]

Finally, a very recent reforms in Mexico City (2011) and Coahuila (2012) has added the creation of so-called 'State Register of Alimony and Children Support Debtors' (compare *infra*, 69).

I. Birth Certificates

24. All people have the obligation to declare the birth of a baby and this responsibility falls precisely onto parents and grandparents, knowing that doctors should also be made aware of the birth, as well as the directors of health establishments, whether private or public.[13]

11. The CCCOAH 2012 has a special registry form that refer to the so-called 'civil solidarity pact' (Art. 147), namely, a legal form of marriage between same-sex couples to provide mutual assistance.
12. In 2004 there have been in place important reforms in this matter (Book One 'Of Persons', Fourth Title 'On Civil Registry'). They mainly are referred to the care of record inscriptions by computer means through a database permitting its preservation and authenticity by using an electronic signature, and to the equivalent value of certified copies (Arts 36 and 48 CCDF); to the possibility to issue partial records of acts (*extractos*, Art. 39); also the necessity of the two witnesses is eliminated (Arts 98 fr. III, 103, fr. VIII, 118 and 119 fr. III); moreover, it is required from Civil Registry judges the duty of send to family judges the official notices (Arts 35, 75, 76, 78, 82, 83, 84, 89 second paragraph, 114–116, 126, 131–133, 291 and 401 CCDF); finally it occurs the same in the opposite way, that is to say, with the family judge legal duty to give to the judge of the registry the corresponding notices about legal sentences related to Civil Registry records (general case of Art. 131 CCDF).
13. Unfortunately, our country maintains still severe insufficiencies in this matter and it had to be recognized recently by the authorities that about eight million Mexicans are not registered with the Civil

This birth certificate must be drawn up in the presence of two witnesses and may refer to a baby born within a marriage or a baby born outside it. In this last case it must not be expressed on the certificate that the baby is a natural child. It is the same case in the event of a baby resulting from an incestuous relationship.

In the event of abandoned babies, there is the obligation of functionaries of the Civil Registry to report all of the circumstances of the case, but it is prohibited to do any paternity inquiry.

Regarding Mexicans born outside the country, it has been established that registration in the local corresponding office of the national territory is necessary:

> Such legal requirement is essential for the plain validation of the referred acts, because it is the form that the legislator, according to the principle of national sovereignty, will establish the way to penalize, by Mexican authority, these kinds of documents coming from outside Mexico with, especially trying to demonstrate with them a fact of public ordeal, as it is the civil status of people.[14]

II. Certificates of Recognition

25. A natural child can be recognized with the simple presentation of the baby before the registration offices. If it concerns an adult, the expressed consent of the adult recognized on the certificate is required.[15]

A child born outside marriage can also be recognized by means of a special certificate before the judge of the Civil Registry, or by public statement before a notary or by testament and even by judicial statement where such circumstance is confessed directly and expressly.

III. Certificates of Adoption

26. As for certificates of adoption, the judge restrains himself or herself to setting down the corresponding certification with the definite judicial resolution authorizing the adoption of the minor or handicapped person.

Registry. In general, the civil codes establish that declarations have to be done in a term of 180 days from the birth date, but in Tabasco the term can be until 365 days from the birth date (Art. 86).

As established in a reform in 2004 (CCDF), now the collateral parents are obligated to declare the birth, always in the term of six months (Art. 55). The ways of proving the birth are, of course, the certificate issued by the authorized doctor in the special forms of Health Secretary. In the case of not having this certificate, a document can be admitted proving the birth, and still not having it because of force majeure, with a denunciation of facts before the ministerial authority (Art. 54).

The references to the *adultery* and *incestuous* children are eliminated (Arts 62 and 64) and also the references to the particularities of births on board of ships – unthinkable in Mexico City – and vehicles (Arts 70–74).

14. Adolfo Rodríguez Dueñas [1977] CIII S.J.F. 155.
15. Due to legal reforms in Mexico City, it has been eliminated the adjective *natural* and they were reinforced the security measures concerning the secret of the birth certificate original and the impossibility of record or any publication, except if it is done by a stated judicial order (Art. 82, 2004).

This kind of certificate can have two variations, depending on it being a *simple* or a *total* adoption. In the first case the names of adoptant and adopted must be written down, as well as those of the people who might have given their acceptance for the adoption and those of the witnesses that may have acted. In this kind of certificate, the most important data about the judicial resolution will be written down.

In the second case the certificate must be settled as if it were a birth certificate, exactly in the same terms as if it were about a child related by blood.[16]

IV. Certificates of Guardianship

27. The functionary at the Civil Registry must in this case settle the corresponding certificate in the specified terms in the act of understanding of the guardianship, containing information about the handicapped person, the kind of incapacity, the tutor's and caretaker's data, the consign warranty and the data of the people who have had the handicapped person under their parental authority, as well as the name of the authority that granted the act.

V. Certificates of Emancipation

28. Emancipation is a phenomenon which results from a minor marriage and it is produced automatically. In these cases it is sufficient if the applicant shows the update of what is assumed before the judge of the Civil Registry presenting the related wedding certificate. The functionary may not need to draw up a separate certificate.

VI. Marriage Certificates

29. As it is the case of a marital link, the judge of the Civil Registry is responsible for a series of formalities that fulfil the degree of solemnity in our law. All of these formalities will be specified in much more depth in the corresponding part to the formalities of marriage (*infra*, paragraph 64).

In terms as set out by Article 103, the judge of the Civil Registry must proceed to settle the marriage certificate where the judge can relate all of the previous circumstances plus the manifestation that the demanded formalities were fulfilled.[17]

---

16. One more time, for Mexico City it is necessary to clarify that it has been already eliminated the double distinction between *simple adoptions* and *total adoptions*, which are still available in other states (cf. *infra* para. 106). Consequently, it was revoked the Art. 88 which only mentioned the simple adoption. Therefore, the Art. 86 prevents to make an act as it were a 'birth date certificate', this is to say, similar to the one which is issued for blood children.
17. Once again in the case of Mexico City, the reforms made in 2004 do not restrict the election of the judge of the Civil Registry, because this official may be elected in absolute freedom (Art. 97). The witnesses are also eliminated, but the fingerprint of pretenders is demanded and the judge is obligated to warn enough about the rights and obligations as a result of the marriage (Art. 102, para. 2nd).

VII. Divorce Certificates

30. The divorce certificate must be settled having the firm statement on sight that declares the resolution of the corresponding link. The functionary of the registry has the obligation to write then the marriage certificate of the divorced in the terms stated in Article 116.

VIII. Death Certificates

31. The death certificate of people must satisfy the requirements of Article 119, that is: Personal data of the dead person, marital status, wife's name, the deceased's parents, the disease that caused death, burial place and precise time of death, and all related circumstances in the case of violent death. In this last hypothesis, however, the Public Prosecutor must be acquainted with the facts.

However, the law explains the details of acts that must be settled in very special cases such as death caused by flood, drowning, fire, or any other accident in general, and disappearance of the corpse.[18]

IX. Certificates of Inscription of Statements that Declare or Modify the Marital Status

32. Another kind of special format is required for the case of inscription of statements that declare or modify the marital status. The intervention of the judge is reduced to make the corresponding writing and to insert the essential data of the respective judicial resolution.

X. Certificates of Correction, Modification and Clearing Up of the Own Certificates of the Registry

33. As a general principle, it is established that the correction or modification of certificates can only be made under consequence of a judicial sentence. The only exceptional case is the parents' voluntary recognition of a child.

The correction or modification by judicial means can only be made in case of falsehood or amendments, either essential mistake or accidental. The correction must be requested by the interested people or by any other person somehow related to the registered act, but it can also be requested by his/her heirs.

---

18. In this case, it has been extended the term of the burial or cremation up to the next forty-eight hours according to the reforms made in 2004 to the Art. 117 and a correlation of the data contained in the death certificate with the data of the related criminal inquiry is demanded (Art. 119, fr. VI). Now, the references to death occurred on board of ships and aircrafts, in military campaign, and the ones of the executed by death penalty, were eliminated (Arts 125, 127 and 128).

The obligation of the registrar is reduced to receiving in his/her terms the resolution and to writing a reference to it in the margin of the questioned certificate, either in a positive or negative sense.

Finally, it is important to mention the existence of a prompted procedure for the clearing up of the certificates when it is about mecanographic mistakes, orthographic or of another kind that may not affect the essential data. In this last case, the correction can be made in the Central Civil Registry's Office.

Chapter 3. Personal Rights

34. The personal rights in our legislation refer to a series of values which do not represent monetary value, but have a moral, affective, or sentimental character. Just the CC of the states of Jalisco, Puebla, Queretaro, and Quintana Roo contain a specific personal rights section that, generally, consignate the personal essential attributes, number the nature and denomination of the protected right establishing the relative exceptions, and consigning that their violation constitutes source of obligations.

Thus, the CC of Morelos deals with them in the Articles 1348, 1348*bis* and 1349, but it does not conform to a special chapter. The CC of Coahuila points out that physical personal rights are the capacity, the name, the address, the nationality, the marital status, the patrimony and the rights to the personality (Article 35). These rights to the personality are honour or reputation; where appropriate, the professional title; aesthetic presence; correspondence, phone, professional, and probate secret; and private or personal life (Article 90 CCCOAH). In the case of moral person (Articles 239 et seq.) the only exceptions refer to the marital status and to the personal rights, which cannot be attributed to this type. In a very recent reform (2010) in the State of Mexico the law states that the rights of natural persons and collective persons are honour, reputation and prestige; private and family life; respect for image and voice copies, name or pseudonym, and personal identity; address, aesthetic presence, affective values from family, friends and property; and physical and psychological integrity (Article 2.5 CCMEX).

All codes consider that the rights of the personality are innate rights, absolute, extrapatrimonial, inalienable, not subject to term, unquittable, capable to oppose the authority and third parties and cannot be disposed of, expropriated, or seized. The code of Jalisco says besides that they are essential, truly subjective, original, and absolute (Article 26).

A relevant topic is the right to make use of one's own body or some part of it for medical aims as a favour towards another person. The possibility that the corpse could be destined for therapeutic, teaching, or investigation aims is also foreseen. With this objective, such disposition must be stated in a written form and communicated to the close relatives, the beneficiary institution and the civil registry.[19]

---

19. It is important to mention, however, that the regulation of some personal rights has been the object of a very recent reformation in the Political Constitution of the State of Veracruz (*Constitución Política del Estado de Veracruz*, CPEV). Thus, is established a Chapter II entitled 'On the human rights' and a specific procedure of protection of them. Specifically, Art. 6 of this chapter says the following:

> The authorities of the State will promote the necessary conditions for the plain possession of freedom, equality, security and non-discrimination of people; also, they will guarantee the right to honor, the personal and family intimacy and the free development of personality.

Besides, Art. 8 mentions the right to live and to grow in a healthy and balanced natural environment, entitling 'all people' to the preservation, restoration and balance of Nature.

The CCDF prevents moral damage in its Article 1916, in the following form:

> By moral harm it is understood the affectation that a person suffers in his feelings, affections, beliefs, decency, honor, reputation, private life, configuration and physical aspects, or in the consideration that the others have of himself. It will be assumed that there was moral harm when psychic of physic integrity or freedom of people is vulnerable or illegally damaged.[20]

The gatering of reformations to the CPEV of 3 Feb. 2000 has earned its provincial judgment as the first modern constitution of the twenty-first century. The actual CPEUM contains no specific disposition about it, although a reformation of 8 May 1999 adds the following paragraph to Art. 4: 'Every person has the right to live in an adequate environment for this development and well-being.'

20. T. Olivera J., *El daño moral* (México: Themis, 1993), 7.

Chapter 4. Names

35. Name is one of the attributions of a person. The right to the name is regulated specifically by the CC of the states of Jalisco, Puebla, Queretaro, Quintana Roo, Tabasco, Veracruz, and Zacatecas, and by the FC of Morelos. Thus, for example, the CCQRO (Article 35) mentions that 'The name is the vocative which is used to designate a person and it will be fixed up by the proper name and the surnames when it is about physical persons'. In the same sense, Article 76 of the CC of Morelos (compare Article 14 FCMOR).

The CCDF does not expressly contain any disposition that may refer expressly to it, but Article 58 states that the birth certificate must contain the name and family names that correspond to the child, along with his digital fingerprint and corresponding sex. Besides, the judge will give the fathers' family names of both parents in the case of children born out of marriage, or if only one of the parents recognizes it, his two family names (Articles 58 and 60).

§1. Composition of a Name (First Name, Surname, Individual Name, Title of Nobility)

36. In other local legislations, specific rules about the formation of a name are to be stated in an express form. In this way, the children of a marriage will bear the proper name or names that their parents give them and next the surname of the father or his and the mother's (e.g., Article 47 CCVER).

37. *Quid iuris* in case of adoption? According to the new Article 395 CCDF, the adopted person must carry the surnames of the adoptant or the adoptants, because the adoption extinguishes the original filiation with the progenitors – except in some cases that will be seen later on (*infra*, paragraph 63, 'impediments of marriage'). The only limitation is that for any circumstance in particular, this legal solution is not considered convenient.

38. There are other specific cases. For example, the foundling or abandoned minors (see *infra,* 125) may carry the name and surnames that are freely given to them, in the terms set in Article 67 CCDF. However, some codes foresee the case of this name coinciding with someone else's. If this is the case, this circumstance might somehow cause harm. In this hypothesis, it is possible to present before the judicial authority and obtain a change of name of the abandoned. If the harmed person manages to prove his right, then the foundling or abandoned person must change his/her name and the judge can freely impose another name on him.

39. As for spouses, any of them can add to his/her own name and surname someone else's surname and in the social practice it is customary even to add the possessive 'of' before the addition.[21] Now, in cases of the breaking up of the marital link, once the statement that dissolves marriage has been executed, the spouse that had adopted the name of the partner cannot continue using it. As in the event of widows or widowers, the law states expressly that the spouse can continue to carry the name of the deceased. It is customary to add the expression of the state of widowhood, even in an abbreviated form ('Vda.', for *viuda*).

40. However, the name corresponding to the moral persons of public character must be shaped precisely to the one foreseen in law. This is the case of the name of the nation, states, municipalities and other institutions of public character. The societies of civil or mercantile character, unions and others, will carry the name or reason foreseen in its corporated chapter, too.

41. It is also appropriate to state here that, apart from the name, a physical person has the right to use, in an exclusive form, pseudonyms, anagrams or mottos.[22] The registry of the same is not compulsory, but the responsible person has the obligation to maintain it and to respond for its inadequate use (Articles 70–74 CCVER).

42. Finally, concerning nobility titles, these are forbidden in the terms stated in Article 12 CPEUM, which states 'In the Mexican United States nobility titles are not granted, nor prerogatives and hereditary honours, nor will it be given any kind of effect to those granted by any other country'. However, such prohibition does not contain the possibility of receiving decorations even from foreign governments, as is foreseen expressly in Article 37 Part b, I and III of the same legal body, with the permission of the General Congress.

§2. Surname

I. Acquisition of the Surname

43. It has been said before that the CCDF does not contain an express chapter which may refer to this topic but, in return it is possible to find, in the dispositions concerning the Civil Registry, some specific rules about the matter. Thus, Article 58 says that the birth certificate must carry the 'name and surnames that correspond' to the presented.

44. The recent dispositions of the CCDF no longer contain the former distinction between 'children born in wedlock' and 'children born out of wedlock'. The codes of the rest of the Republic show several possibilities that are presented here. First, if the child is a 'child born in wedlock', the law demands that the names,

21. In Coahuila the new CC states that the fact of a spouse adding the last name of his spouse will not make any legal effect (Art. 67), but still in Jalisco the CC of 1995 permits it (Art. 65), even eliminating spouse's last names.
22. In a contrary sense, the FC of Morelos (Art. 15) mentions that it is not allowed to use nicknames at the conclusion of the legal civilians acts. His contravention occurs on the nullity of the act. It is the same case in the state of Guanajuato, according to Art. 68, I, b, since December 2011.

address and nationality of the parents and even the corresponding data to grandparents be registered. Thus, the surname of parents is transmitted automatically to the child according to the stated rules in the final part of Article 58 CCDF 'The Judge will put the paternal surname of the parents.' Therefore, at the moment of the presentation the maternal surnames of both parents are lost automatically and they do not transcend to the minor.[23]

45. The second possibility within provincial codes refers to the presentation of a baby as if it were a 'child born out of wedlock'. This special case constitutes a hypothesis of exception to the general rule contained in Article 58 *in fine*, because it is stated expressly that he/she must carry the two surnames of those who might recognize him/her.

46. The third and last possibility refers, diversely, to the presentation of an abandoned child from unknown parents because then the judge of the Civil Registry has the faculty to give the name and the surnames that the judge might consider convenient.

II. Change of the Surname

47. By general rule, change of name and surname is not permitted to any *person*. This is the categorical statement, for example, of Article 63 CC of Jalisco. Indeed, the CC of the Federal District does not accept in this aspect rectifications, modifications, or clarifications of birth certificates neither in voluntary trials nor notarial deeds declarations (Article 138*bis*, *in fine* CCDF). Furthermore, a recent judgment of the Supreme Court of Justice solved that the modification of a person's surname only can proceed if it is necessary to adjust it at the social reality, taking as foundation the so-called 'principle of immutability'.[24]

Nevertheless, in some other codes of the Republic it has been stated legislatively the possibility to change name and surname only by certain and closed causes. Those are, for example, the cases of the CC of the states of Quintana Roo (Article 546), Tabasco (Article 54), Puebla (Article 70), and Jalisco (Article 64), that expressly foresee the modification by the invariable and constant use of another different name, by the exposition to ridicule, and in the case of homonymia. Furthermore, in Veracruz a person can change his name and surname quiet simply for a voluntary cause, even in a notary's venue and notifying the change to the Civil Registry. This is the text of Article 61 CCVER:

The change of name will proceed:

(i) In cases of homonymia, in order that the physical person or the moral person who subsequently acquired the name stop using the homonymous one.

23. Cf. e.g. Art. 68, II, a), CCGTO, 2011.
24. This statement has not been listed yet in the official publication. The preliminary identification data are: Direct Appeal in review 259/2013 (23 Oct. 2013). Speaker: Jorge Mario Pardo Rebolledo. Secretary: José Díaz de León Cruz.

(ii) When in a voluntary form a person decides to change the name, with the appropriate publicity and heard by any person who can be injured for this act.

48. The CPCVER in its Articles 503–505 signals carefully the procedure for the change of name. The procedure starts with a request from the interested party; once this is done, and received by the tribunal, it must be published in an extract three times in a row in the state's official newspaper, in a local newspaper, and in the tribunal bulletin board. It is granted a term of fifteen days immediately after the last publication for any opposition to be presented. If there were any, it must sustain ordinary trial in the terms foreseen by the same code.

If there are no claims after this term, the procedure is then turned to the social representation, where the public ministry must state its opinion, according to Article 67 CC of Veracruz. Once the favourable opinion of the representation is conceded, the procedure is turned to the judge once again for it to be dictated a resolution. When the resolution is pronounced and there are no ulterior resources, it is drawn up as a certified copy that is sent to the person in charge of the civil registry. This same resolution is published once again in the state's official newspaper, in a local newspaper, and in the tribunal bulletin board.

It is important to state that even when the person modifies his/her name, such modification does not release or exempt him/her from the obligations or responsibilities contracted with the former name.

49. As for moral persons, the statute or constitutive minutes must be analysed previously, in the hypothesis that they may contain specific dispositions about it. This kind of person must carry a special registry in the public offices with respect to all of the changes that may affect his/her social denomination.

In the judicial practice, there is controversy with respect to the possibility that only the proper name of the physical person can be changed, this means, the appellative, or the name plus the surnames.

The first view point states that the change of name does not authorize the changing of surnames, because the first one is imposed by parents – and by exception by other people – and as for the surnames there are precise rules for their formation, which are imperative norms and of public interest, because by authorizing such change, it would imply a modification in the filiation. This is the case of Article 138, I, II, CCGTO, December 2011.

However, the second view point states that the change of name includes not only the proper name, but also the surnames, because by talking about name it is referring to the totality of the same, that means the proper name and the surnames that constitute the complete and correct name of a person, as it was stated before.

§3. First Name

50. In the colloquial language of our country it is customary to call *nombre de pila* to the first name – or names – that a person carries, whose concept does not make reference to the addition of paternal or maternal surnames and, therefore, they configurate a restricted version of the appellative. In fact, it is possible even to find a dogmatic support, for instance in Article 47 of the CCVER that literally says that the children born from marriage 'will carry the name or same names that their parents impose to them, followed by the surname'.

This curious denomination of *nombre de pila* makes reference of course to the appellative that parents impose according to the religious tradition of taking the babies to the Catholic ceremony of the baptism and specially to the bathing with holy water that the newborn receives as the priest pronounces the sacramental words that mean his entry as a son of God, at the time that he supports his left hand on the head of the minor.

The denomination of proper name that utilizes the civil legislation, surely expresses the difference that can be found in the fact that this name concerns only to the child, as the surnames are necessarily shared with the parents.

Anyway, it is curious to see that a very deep-rooted Mexican custom transmits quite often to the baby even the same name of the parents, keeping only the distinction of the gender.

Finally, it must be signalled the rather extensive custom in Mexico of imposing on the new born not only one proper name or *de pila*, but also two or three, frequently as a tribute to the Virgin or some saint from the Catholic calendar, with which the complete name of the minor adopts a great typical extension in the Hispanic names. Guanajuato is a notable exception, because a recent legislative reform, in 2011 (Article 68, fr. I, a, CCGTO), states that in the imposition of proper name, there will only be a traditional Hispanic composed name (e.g., José Antonio, María de Lourdes) or until two new names (e.g., Jonathan Kevin, Mario Ricardo).

Chapter 5. Nationality

51. Nationality is another attribute of people. Nationality establishes one's attachment to a determined country and, with it, a series of rights and obligations.

Regarding nationality, our Constitution applies. Effectively, in Articles 30 et seq. of this legal body, it is established that Mexican nationality is acquired by birth or by naturalization. As for the birth, such prerogative is conferred by the simple fact of birth in the territory of the Republic, regardless of the parents' nationality. It is also conceded to those who are born outside Mexico with Mexican parents, or at least one of them has this characteristic. Finally, to those who are born on board of Mexican aircrafts or ships, independently from the nationality of their parents.

However, Mexicans by naturalization are foreigners that may receive the corresponding document (naturalization letter) from the respective dependence, which in this case is the Foreign Relations Secretary. Mexicans by naturalization are also the women or men of foreign nationality, who marry a Mexican person and then establish their address in the national territory.

52. The Mexican nationality carries, along with the prerogatives that it offers, also a group of obligations such as children receiving civic and military education, as well as general education of primary character and secondary, to register in the National Guard and, finally, to contribute to the public expenses.

The prerogatives that all Mexican citizens have refer, among others, to the right to vote and to be elected; to take part in political matters; to enrol in the National Army; to exercise the right of petition; to be appointed to any public service; and vote in referendums on issues of national importance (Article 35 CPEUM).

53. However, there are some reasons for the loss of nationality and citizenship. The first case is foreseen in Article 37 CPEUM that mentions that any Mexican by birth may be deprived of his nationality but nationality by naturalization can be loss with the voluntary acquisition of a foreign nationality, and for living five years continuously abroad. The second case refers to the loss of citizenship, listing the following causes: acceptance or use of nobility titles of foreign governments; by voluntarily provide services or official duties to a foreign government; acceptance or use of foreign awards; accepting other countries titles or functions (except for literary, scientific or humanitarian titles), and to help a foreign citizen or government on a diplomatic claim or in an international tribunal, against the nation (compare Articles 27–32, Nationality Law [Ley *de Nacionalidad*, LN, 1998, with reforms until April 2012]).

There is also the Article 86 LGP that displays the creation of a Population's National Registry (*Registro Nacional de Población*) which has the objective to register every person who might integrate into the population of the country, with true data that permit the certification and credit their identity. In this Population's National Registry must be included Mexicans and foreigners as well, with a code of the Population's Registry's Unique Key already mentioned, that registers and identifies the person in an exclusive way.

Thus, this registry prepares the expedition of the Citizen's Identity Document (*Cédula de Identidad Ciudadana*, CIC), but at the time of revision of this monograph, this document does not exist yet. In the terms stated in Article 104 LGP, this document must become the official document of identification and in its own terms, it will plainly prove the identity data that it may contain in relation to its titular holder. These data are the paternal surname, maternal surname and name(s); the population's Registry's Unique Key; the title holder's photograph; birthplace; birth date; and signature and fingerprint.

Chapter 6. Domicile and Residence

54. Another of the essential attributes of a person is the *domicilio*. The word *domicilio* (address) comes from the Latin word *domus* which means house or dwelling.[25]

The address of the physical person is the place where he lives in a habitual form. If this 'habitual residence' does not take place in practice, then the place where the person maintains the main seat of his business is considered. Only if one or the other is missing, the place where the person finds himself is taken into account. In this case, there is also the assumption that establishes that a person lives 'habitually' in a place when he remains in it for more than six months (Article 29 CCDF).

The doctrine also distinguishes the *legal address* of a person. By legal address is understood the address that the law recognizes for a person's exercising his rights and fulfilling his/her obligations. It results, as it is seen, in a fiction, because it does not necessarily have to coincide with the physical presence of the same. Starting from this hypothesis, Article 31 of the CCDF establishes a series of specific assumptions for the designation of the legal address. So, it is recognized as a legal address that of the under-aged not emancipated, the one of the person whose parental custody he is subjected to; of the under-aged who is not under the parental custody, or if the under-aged is handicapped, or for the minors or abandoned handicapped, that of his tutor; of the spouses, that in which these live; of the military, the place where they are destined; of the public servers, the place where they carry out their functions; of those sentenced to suffer a penalty of deprivation of freedom for more than six months, the city where it is the jail.

55. Let us take a brief look now at the case of the address of moral people. At this point, Article 33 CCDF establishes that moral persons have their address in the place where their administration is established; that is, what now is known as the headquarters of the corporative offices of an enterprise. Here there are assumptions, as well, as is the case in considering the local address of foreign moral persons who execute juridical acts in the region. The same happens in the case of branches offices, because the place where they carry out operations is considered as a legal address, although it may not coincide with the address of the headquarters.

As is seen, the concept 'address' involves the *residence*, either in a physical sense, or in a legal assuming sense, in the case of physical persons as well as that of moral persons.

---

25. The CC of the State of Zacatecas gives a definition in general terms in its Art. 37 which says: 'The address is the place that is fixed to people for the normal fulfilling of their obligations and for the exercise of their rights.'

However, an old statement has determined that the main elements to determine the address are 'The constant residence and the main seat of business, joined at will of staying in the place where one resides' (Hacienda Pública de Veracruz [1965] XXVIII S.J.F. 2265).

56. Finally, it is important to say that some codes (compare e.g., Article 43 CCVER) even distinguish the concept of *neighbourhood* (*vecindad*), which consists of the simple personal residence in the local territorial area of the respective legislation (Veracruz state, in this case).

Chapter 7. Mentally Handicapped Persons

57. We have already seen (*supra*, paragraph 18) that the civil legislation establishes in an expressed form the causes of incapacity that it divides then into civil and natural causes (Article 450 CCDF). This disposition contains one of the most advanced formulations in the matter. Unfortunately, until recently some other local codes still referred to this kind of incapacity with qualifiers that carried out a certain discrimination towards these people ('privates of intelligence by madness, idiotism or imbecility').

A disabled person from the mental point of view requires the protection of law. In this case, the Code has a specific procedure to declare the state of interdiction of the person, which we have already mentioned in a former paragraph (*supra*, paragraph 19).

58. The declaration of interdiction of a person must follow a procedure in the terms set out in the Civil Procedures Code of the Federal District (CPCDF), which establish a voluntary trial for the naming of tutors and caretakers and the understanding of the charges under consequence of the state of minority or disability of the person, in the terms foreseen by Article 450 of the CCDF. The resulting procedure is quick and expeditious, although different circumstances might appear in its execution.

However, it is quite clear that the declaration of incapacity by madness must be followed in an ordinary trial with all of the necessary formalities, with a very detailed procedure that incorporates harmful procedures for the protection of the sick, medical revision by experts, and the corresponding judgment. The procedure is found carefully foreseen in Articles 902–914 CPCDF.

59. The acts celebrated by the interdict are considered void, in terms set out in Article 635 of the CCDF. In this event, this voidness must be recognized as relative, because it can only be discussed by the disabled– once recovered from his incapacity – or by his legitimate representatives and precisely in the prescribed term for the real or personal actions, according to the nature of the act. Thus, this disposition, that is stated in Article 638, must relate to Articles 1159 and 1161–1162, although it is convenient to declare, that even being applicable, none of these precepts has the distinction of the prescription period for real or personal actions and, if so, Article 1162 grants the same period (five years) for the charging of periodical benefits, regardless of their coming from real or personal actions.

Nevertheless, all of these cases show two remarkable exceptions: first, if the under-aged are experts of the subject in the business they are dealing with; and second, if they try to prove that they are adults using fake certificates (Articles 639–640 CCDF).

In the last years, due to the political alternations which have occurred in our country and to the plural conformation of Federal Congress, they have been issued several new laws incorporating ostensible advances in several aspects. As an example they can be shown:

- Law to protect small girls, small boys and adolescents (*Diario Oficial de la Federación*, 29 May 2000).
- Law of the rights of indigenous peoples and communities in the State of Oaxaca (*Periódico Oficial*, 19 June 1998, reformed on 15 September 2001).
- Law of the rights of Old Age Adults in Federal District (*Diario Oficial de la Federación*, 25 June 2002).[26]
- Law of the rights of Old Age Adults in the State of Nuevo León (*Periódico Oficial*, 7 January 2005).
- Law to prevent and punish the slave trade (*Diario Oficial de la Federación*, 27 November 2007).
- Law of the Old Age Adults of State of Mexico (*Gaceta del Gobierno,* 6 August 2008).
- Law of the rights of Old Age Adults of the State of Veracruz (*Gaceta Oficial,* 31 July 2013).

26. In this particular case, the law orders to create a unique register of orphanage, hostels, residences, asylums, accommodations, shelters, or inns. The statistics aggravate to become shocking, since it is estimated that in 2014 there are 10.9 millions and in 2030 there probably will be 22.0 million. A law in Jalisco state takes particularly into account the circumstances of the incapacity, senescence, culture, and social condition of persons (Art. 1st CCJAL).

Part II. Family Law

Chapter 1. Marriage

§1. The Nature of Marriage

60. There is, as it is known, a large controversy over the juridical nature of the matrimonial institution. It has been said, thus, that it is a sacrament, an institution, a contract, etc.

Indeed, some civil codes typify marriage as a 'social and civil institution' (Veracruz, Querétaro, Hidalgo, Jalisco, Baja California), but others simply state it as a 'contract' (Puebla and Oaxaca), or 'a community of life' (Federal District).

However, our supreme federal legislation had tactfully solved the problem stating in Article 130 (CPEUM) that marriage in our country constitutes a 'civil contract.' Nevertheless, ever since the important reformations that took place in recent times, such affirmation seems unnecessary and it has to do, of course, with the historical separation that has existed between the State and the church. Certainly, Article 130 CPEUM establishes now that the marital status acts are of the exclusive competence of the governmental authorities and not more of church authorities.

However, a reformation in June 2000 in the CCDF foresees expressly the governmental protection for the organization and the integral development of family members, as well as respect for its dignity. In this same reformation the term 'familiar juridical relations' is defined as 'the gathering of rights and duties of the people part of the family'. Its regulation is of public and social interest.[27]

It is important to state here that these familiar juridical relations now have their source in three different institutions, which are marriage, kinship and concubinage.

61. Some codes also define marriage. Among them, the CCVER in its Article 75 states that 'Marriage is the union of a single man and a single woman that convive to carry out the essential aims of the family as a social and a civil institution' (compare too Article 294 CCPUE). This had been until recently the traditional definition, but for the CCDF the institution is now defined in Article 146: 'Marriage is the free union of *two people* to do the community of life, were both give respect to each

27. The same reform in 2000 has eliminated the entire chapter concerning the betrothal, that is to say, the formal courtship that, in general, precedes the marriage, through the correspondent promise (Arts 139–145). The same occurred in Puebla (Art. 295), Sinaloa (Arts 139–145) and Coahuila, where at present 'Any agreement of betrothal, whichever the name to call it, will not make any legal effect' (Art. 253). To the contrary, the new FCMOR (2006) stills conserves the figure (Art. 66).

other, equity and mutual help. It must be celebrated before the judge of the Civil Registry and with the formalities that this law demands.'[28]

The new Law of Society of Coexistence for Mexico City, 2006 (*Ley de Sociedades de Convivencia*), allows already the marriage between two physical persons of different sex or of the same-sex, being of age and with full legal capacity. It also admits the concession of alimony, pensions, special testamentary dispositions, repairs on patrimony damages, moral damages and social benefits, but it does not permit to adopt in a global nor individual form.

The same happened in Coahuila with the named 'Civil Agreement of Solidarity', which consists in a contract celebrated by two persons, of the same or different sex, in order to organize their common lives. The partners celebrating this agreement are considered 'civil mates' (Articles 385-1 a 385-8 CCCOAH, 2007).

Finally, in October 2013 it was enacted the Free Living Together Law of the Jalisco State (*Ley de Libre Convivencia*), very similar to the last one. This 'free living together' requires execution before a notary public. There is no possibility to adopt.

But, however, recently in 2010 the State of Mexico has reaffirmed the marriage traditional features stating that 'marriage is a public institution and social interest, through which *a man and a woman* voluntarily decide to share a life estate for search for personal fulfilment and the foundation of a family' (Article 4.1*bis* CCMEX).

§2. The Capacity to Marry

62. The marital contract carries out a series of requirements that are found in detail in the legislation. The law establishes a minimal age for contracting marriage. So, the CC of Federal District (Article 148, 2004), Guerrero (Article 412), Coahuila (Article 255), and the FC of Hidalgo (Article 30 fr. II), raise this minimal age to 18 years old, but exceptionally demand only 16 (in both male and female) with previous authorization of their parent; supposing that the parents may not be alive, the consent of the tutors, and in an extreme case, a judge of the family affairs consent must be obtained.[29]

---

28. It is not common that the civil codes define the concept of family. However, the CC of the states of Jalisco (Art. 778), Aguascalientes (Art. 747), Quintana Roo (Art. 1190), Tamaulipas (Art. 663), Michoacán (Art. 120 [cf. Art. 1st FCMICH]), Queretaro (Art. 135), Guerrero (Art. 374), the FCZAC (Art. 3rd) and Hidalgo (Art. 340) in fact contain dogmatically a definition of family. There are even in motivate definitions which can be found in the new family laws of Zacatecas, Yucatan, Morelos, Hidalgo, and Michoacan states.

    Basically, a family is conceived as an institution socio-political, formed by a group of people, unified by the parental relationship, the marriage, or the concubinage, to which is attributed a juridical personality. This is the general sense of the Arts 3rd, FCZAC; 2nd, FCYUC; 22, FCMOR; 2nd, FCHGO; 1st, FCMICH, and 2nd, FCSIN. It is necessary to mention that the CCMOR, in its Art. 120 (cf. Art. 22 FCMOR) states that 'Family in the state of Morelos is a natural association.'
29. A very recent reform in Veracruz (Art. 86, February 2014) have not exceptions.

    The states of Puebla (Art. 300), Jalisco (Art. 260) and Nuevo Leon (Art. 148, since 2011) demand the same age in both spouses, but set at 16 years; meanwhile, the CCBCS (Art. 157) demands the age of 18 years in the male and 16 in the female.

63. The Code establishes an extensive list of *impediments* to celebrate the contract of marriage. According to new Article 156 CCDF, they are the lack of minimal age; the lack of consent from parents, or tutor, or family judge; the consanguinity, affinity and civil kinship; the adultery; the attempt against the life of any of the married in order to contract marriage with the widow or widower; the physical or moral violence to celebrate the marriage; the incurable impotence for the copulation; the chronic, incurable, contagious, and hereditary diseases; the physical or mental incapacity; and a previous marriage with a different person.

The consanguinity kinship is a serious impediment, either lineal or collateral without limitation of degree in a straight line, ascendant or descendant. In the even collateral line, the impediment includes brothers and step brothers. In the uneven collateral, the impediment includes only uncles and nephews, as long as they are in the third degree and they have not obtained an exception. The affinity kinship is an impediment in a straight line, without any limitation. Finally, the civil kinship resulting from adoption is now considered in Mexico City and others provincial codes as a blood kinship.

§3. Formalities of Marriage

64. It has been said above (*supra*, paragraph 61) that the CCDF is explicit in the sense that marriage contract must be celebrated in the presence of certain functionaries and precisely with the formalities – or solemnities – that law demands. It is necessary to present an application with the information foreseen by Article 97, that is reduced to the following: general data of those people requesting and general data of their parents; expressed declaration that they do not have any legal impediment to marry and finally, that it is their free will to join in marriage.

This writing must be signed by those requesting and must include birth certificates or a medical certificate to credit their ages, the consent that the ascendants, tutors or authorities give, declaration of two witnesses, medical certification, agreement with relation to the assets and regime of these and, if necessary, a copy of the death certificate of the previous spouse and a declaration of impediments, must be attached to it.

With this information the judge asks for recognition of the signatures, appointing then the date of the union that must take account of the presence of those interested, witnesses and representatives, if that is the case. In such ceremony the judge proceeds to read out loud the marriage request, the presented documents, etc., then asking the witnesses and spouses if they correspond.

Even the multiple celebrations of marriages in no way exempts the judge from the written fulfilment of the solemnities that are referred to in the former articles (Article 103*bis* CCDF).

The law takes special provisions for the eventual case that the spouses declare a false fact with malice, that the witnesses state any harmful declaration or identity and that doctors act falsely in the expedition of the certificate (Article 104).[30]

30. Some provincial codes demand the previous attendance to the so called 'talks on pre-marriage orientation', among them the FCZAC (Art. 106, 2004), CCJAL (Arts 267*bis* and 268, fr. X, 2008),

65. At this point the legislative provision concerning legal impediments that may occur precisely at the moment of the celebration of marriage is also important. Accusations of impediment may be made by anybody and they have the effect of suspending all latter procedures to settle immediately a certificate stating the circumstances of the case. This certificate must be given immediately to the judge of first instance so he/she can qualify the impediment. The accusations may even be of anonymous character, although of course the judge must take special precautions in verifying.

In any case, the main thing is that once the impediment has been claimed, marriage cannot be celebrated until pronouncement of the judicial decision, concerning its authenticity, one way or the other.

66. It must finally be clarified that as far as Mexicans who get married outside Mexico are concerned, the respective certificate must be registered in the municipalities where they have their new domicile. It concerns, therefore, an efficiency requirement to judge the retroactivity of the consequences of the act. A statement from 1997 from the federal tribunals has interpreted that the expression 'Mexicans who get married outside Mexico' actually means that one of the partners may be of Mexican nationality, that is, that they do not necessarily both have to be Mexicans, because otherwise, they would 'be excluded of their regulation and application to the marriages celebrated outside Mexico, by a national with a foreigner, establishing an exception to such general rule that the merit disposition does not foresee'.[31]

However, other decisions have solved this problem with specific criteria. Thus, a sentence of 1973 states that:

> It results unconceivable that the lack of transcription of the certificate of marriage celebrated outside Mexico brings up the consequence of ignoring in the territory of Veracruz the existence of the marital link … Marriage is a contract of complex juridical effects: Some of familiar or moral ordeal, derived from the nature itself of marriage as a social and civil institution, that produces independently from the transcription of the respective certificate; and others, of patrimonial character, in relation to the juridical acts that the spouses celebrate with third parties and that derive from the knowledge that these have of the marital status of those; knowledge, that is acquired through the pub licity that is given to marriage by means of the transcription of the certificate in the Civil Registry of the place where the spouses are domiciled.[32]

This opinion reinforces itself with another 1983 sentence that states:

> The Certificate of marriage celebrated by Mexicans outside Mexico … in certified copy duly legalized by the diplomatic or consular authorities …

CCVER (Art. 726, fr. IV, 2008), CCQRO (Art. 139*bis*, 2011), CCGTO (Art. 103, since 2012), and FCSIN (Art. 57, fr. 9, 2013). In the state of Yucatan there are the so-named 'parents school' (Arts 1st, II, and 15-16, Law for the Protection of the Family).

31. Succession of Santiago Méndez Suárez [1997] V S.J.F. 763.
32. Leonardo Fernández Cossío [1973] CLXXV S.J.F. 201.

> accompanied by its corresponding translation … has plain proven efficiency … and therefore it is ideal to credit that marital status … lacking importance if it is not registered in thc Civil Rcgistry's office of some place of the Mexican Republic … because that omission only operates in relation to the juridical acts of patrimonial feature that the spouses may perform with third parties, but not into the marital relationship.[33]

§4. Effects of Marriage

67. Once the marital link has been established, the juridical situation displays a series of very complex effects that involve the spouses and, eventually, the children produced from that union.

From the first point of view, the obligation to provide for the economical needs of the marriage is borne between the spouses, contributing to the aims of the marital union and to the obligation of mutual aid. An important part in the fulfilling of this marital aim resides in the conjugal obligation of living together, that is, to make a life in common. For such effect, the law defines the concept of marital domicile, which responds precisely to the house where both decide to live, except in the case of very specific circumstances that the law also foresees. In such sense, the Constitution establishes the right to enjoy a pleasant and dignified home (Article 4 CPEUM, see paragraph 6).

From the legal point of view and based on that foreseen in the Article 4 of the CPEUM, male and female are equal before the law. Therefore, both spouses maintain authority and equal considerations, under the terms set out in Article 168 of the CCDF. The rights and obligations that arise from marriage will always be the same for both spouses and it must be specially observed that the conjunction of these rights and obligations does not depend in any case on the economical contribution to the home's sustenance.[34]

68. Let us see now the effects that, by virtue of marriage, are established in relation to children. In this case, the law foresees specifically from the CPEUM, that laws will protect the organization and the development of the family, stating in addition, that every person has the right to decide about the number and the timing of his or her children. In this same precept, it is also added that it is a duty of parents

33. Enedina Zarazúa Viuda de Contreras [1983] CLXXV S.J.F. 111. The reforms in 2000 to the Art. 161 are still demanding the record transcription of the certificate in the three months starting from the arrival of the couple to Mexico City. The retroactive effects are not mentioned.
34. As for the rights and obligations that are borne out of marriage, it is interesting to consignate that a good number of civil codes in the Republic foresee in an expressed form the duty of fidelity as one of the most important. This is the case of the FC of the states of Hidalgo (Art. 45), Zacatecas (Art. 121); and the case of the CC of Aguascalientes (Art. 158), Tlaxcala (Art. 52), Quintana Roo (Art. 706), Veracruz (Art. 98), Puebla (Art. 314), Morelos (Art. 132 [cf. Art. 84 FCMOR]), Michoacán (Art. 123 FCMICH), Tabasco (Art. 165), Oaxaca (Art. 161) and Yucatan (Art. 83). It should be mentioned by its importance, the Art. 279 of CC of Jalisco that precisely states: 'It is duty and obligation of the spouses, the sexual and affective fidelity.'

to preserve the right of minors to the satisfaction of their necessities and of mental and physical health (Article 4 CPEUM, see paragraph 6).

However, the CCDF following at this point what our Constitution states, says that the right to decide about the number and timing of children, will be exercised in a common agreement by both spouses, under the legal principle of the same authority inside marriage.

In the matter of maintenance provision, the spouses and children have a preferred right over properties and over the economical earnings from whoever sustains economically the family nucleus. The Code is clear about the determination of who has the right to provide this legal duty, because this obligation is borne between the spouses, and between the parents in relation to children – as well as the inverse. Only in the case of absence or impossibility of ascendants or descendants does the obligation fall upon the closest collaterals, that is, the brothers and, in extreme circumstances, in any collateral relative to the fourth degree.

The wide and generous concept that the Code gives to the terms alimony and children support, according to the stated in the new Article 308, comprehends the food, the dressing, the housing, the medical attention, the hospitalizing and in its case, the expenses of pregnancy and childbirth; also, the expenses for minors education and to afford them duty, art, or profession; their habilitation or rehabilitation in case of need; and geriatric attention in case of mentally or physically incapable, or elderly persons.

Some other codes add to this wide concept the attention to the psychic, affective, or healthy fun necessities, and funeral expenses (Article 439 CCJAL), as well as the necessary expenses for books and study material until obtaining an academic degree (Articles 497 and 499 CCPUE; Article 451 CCBCS and Article 473 CCSON), and even recreational needs (Article 206 FCSIN).

It has been established that dependants have the right to acquire child support until reaching the age of 18 years; but in some cases the possibility exists to extend this age limit in practice. Thus, judges must take into consideration all personal circumstances that surround the case to be decided in consequence, because just obtaining a professional title demands from the young person to achieve, as a minimum, the 22 or 23 years-old.

Federal statements of 1996 and 2006 reason in the following sense:

> because of the fact that children support is of public importance, it must be taken into consideration that the very fact of becoming of age must not suspend the obligation to them, but in every case, the circumstances must be examined where siblings reach that age, to find out they are still in need.

If the person that request children support has already finished college, his or her action will be inadmissible even if he or she is studying a master, because those studies are only for specialization. At the same time the circumstance of finishing college studies means that this person is already capable of paying for his or her own support and a master degree.[35]

Because of this, Article 314 of the CCDF limits the food obligation solely to the possibility of acquisition of the duty, art or profession, without compromising supplying siblings with the capital to exercise it.

In practice, however, a way of habitual fulfilling child support lies in the simple fact of incorporating the creditor to the debtor's domicile, in which case the payment for welfare cannot be demanded, except where there is any legal inconvenience or where it is about divorced spouses.[36]

69. As a general rule, it is established in matters of the right to alimony and children support, certain *principles* that must be appointed here. The first principle refers to the reciprocity of the feeding obligation. Such disposition comes as a result of the justice that in itself demands in the solidarity duty to help the one who does not have. The law says, certainly, that the one who gives food also has the right to ask for it.

A second important principle is reduced to the axiom that states that alimony must be given according to the economical possibilities of the person who must provide it and to the vital necessities of those who must receive it. In this form, such axiom establishes a fair principle of proportionality that cannot demand more of the one who does not have or give too much to the one who is in need.

A third principle deals with the number of persons to whom the alimentary obligation applies. In this case, a numerical principle of equality demands that, if everyone had the possibility to do it, the amount of the obligation must be precisely in proportion to their possibilities.

The person who has action to ask for the insurance of alimony is, of course, the own food creditor, but it could also be the ascendant to whose charge the parental custody is found. If there is a tutor, he/she has the obligation to exercise the corresponding action and in the extreme cases the brothers and other collateral relatives within the fourth degree and even the public ministry as a representative of the social interest. The law foresees that the insurance can consist of any warranty form that is sufficient to cover the alimentary expenses, either consisting of a mortgage, pledge, deposit, numerical deposit, etc.

By the way, in Mexico City and in Coahuila the 'State Register of Alimony and Children Support Debtors' have been established (Articles 35, 309 and 323*septimus* CCDF, 2011; Articles 97, 145 and 415, CCCOAH, 2012). People who have failed to comply with their alimony and children support obligations for a period of three months are listed.

---

35. Gustavo Maya Becerril [1996] III S.J.F. 535. The new reforms in Queretaro (Art. 293, 2012) extend the limit until 25-year old students. Cf. in this same sense, Direct Appeal 452/2006 [2007] XXV S.J.F. 1608.
36. The reforms in 2000 and 2005 establish now the obligation to report the need of aliments to the Public Prosecutor or to the family judge (Art. 315*bis* CCDF). These obligations of reporting get now the officials who had to give information on the economical capacity to the food debtors and the employers who refuse to obey the orders of discount (Art. 323, para. 3rd).

70. When does the obligation to give alimony and children support must *cease*? It is evident that one of the first causes of termination of this obligation lies, unfortunately, in the impossibility to satisfy it, that is, when the debtor lacks absolutely the means to fulfil his obligation, which occurs frequently in a country where the percentage of poverty is unfortunately rather high.

On the contrary, the obligation of giving alimony ceases as well when the creditor is no longer in need of it. It is necessary to recognize that between this possibility and that formerly mentioned reside the majority of the cases of alimentary conflicts.

However, there are other causes that result in the cessation of this juridical obligation. It is the case of forthcoming acts that consist in injuries, faults or serious harms that the own creditor alimentary infers to the person who has at his or her charge the feeding obligation, because in such case a sane interpretation of the principle of reciprocity invokes immediately the necessity to suspend the supplying of aliments.

In the same sense the obligation ceases because of a vicious conduct of the feeding creditor, but only as long as such thing happens, because once the cause has been eliminated, the duty of solidarity that sustains the obligation imposes the necessity to satisfy it again in order to, this way, not to perpetuate viciously irregular conduct.

In accordance with that stated in the Article 309 CCDF, it is obvious that the obligation must also cease in the event that the feeding creditor abandons the home where he or she was integrated with the debtor, as long as no justified causes are found.

Finally, according to new reforms in the State of Mexico and in the Coahuila state, the alimony right ceases when the creditor enters into a new marriage, decides to join in concubinage with another person, concludes a 'civil solidarity pact' (*supra,* note 11), or a number of years has elapsed equal to the duration of marriage (Articles 4.99 and 4.109 CCMEX, and 367 CCCOAH).

§5. Void and Voidable Marriages

71. We have already said (*supra*, paragraph 63) that the requirements to get married include the absence of impediments in its celebration. These impediments are listed extensively in Article 156 CCDF. The doctrine shows agreement in recognizing that these causes are divided into *dissolved* impediments and *hindrance* impediments.

The first one, dissolved, refers to the fact that their transgression voids the marital union; the hindrance, instead, possesses as a characteristic the circumstance that its transgression does not void the marriage, but just provoke the illegality of it –besides all other sanctions.[37]

37. However, because of the 2000 reforms in Mexico City, the Arts 264 and 265 have been repealed. It did not happen the same in other provincial codes where the distinction still occurs (Arts 360 CCCOAH, 253 FCMICH and 173 FCMOR).

If any of those impediments happen in the act of celebration of marriage, the juridical act comes void. This is stated expressly in Article 235 CCDF when it says that it is cause of voidness in the celebration of marriage occurring as a result of something of the impediments numbered in Article 156, except in case of previous authorization. Another cause of voidness is marriage has been celebrated in opposition to law (Articles 97, 98, 100, 102 and 103). These Articles refer respectively to the observance of a sort of formalities that we have already analysed in another part (*supra*, paragraph 64).

72. It must be said that as far as foreigners are concerned, the marriage celebrated abroad will always be valid in the country:

> because in this subject it is unanimously accepted the rule of international private law *locus regit actum*, when there is conflict of laws between two nations, that is, that the applicable law as for the form is the one from the place where the act is celebrated ... Therefore, in reference to the limits of application, law, as for the origin or birth of the act, is extraterritorial, because the personal statute of the married follows them everywhere ... the marriage celebrated between foreigners and outside Mexico, valid according to the laws of the country where it is concerted, will apply all of its legal effects in the local federative entity.[38]

In this same sense, a sentence of 1996 has determined also that:

> as for the voidness of the contract of marriage, celebrated under the laws of a foreign country, the judicial authority of the State of Mexico lacks faculties to judge its legality ... In consequence, if a tribunal of this entity determines the voidness of marriage celebrated in a foreign country, it trespasses its sovereignty, because that act was subjected to the laws of the same.[39]

73. The law expressly establishes a diverse cause of voidness when it refers to the concurrence of error from the person the marriage is being contracted with. This kind of error, certainly, breeds a peculiar action of voidness, because it can only be invoked by the offended spouse; although, if the victim does not accuse the error immediately, the voidness causal is as extinguished and the Code declares *iure et de iure* the ratification of the consent – unless there may be another impediment.

Here is, finally, the narration of a very singular case which occurred in Baja California, that has a relation with that stated in Articles 156 fr. XI, and 235 fr. II, CCDF (Article 153 fr. X, CCBC) and that refers to the impediment to celebrate the contract of marriage being subsistent to a previous marriage 'with a different person from the one that it was originally bound to be'. Two people married one to the other, by circumstantial cases, celebrate marriage to each other again, without dissolving the previous link. What happens in this case? A federal tribunal decided the following:

38. Juan Gari Pallares and others [1968] CXXVIII S.J.F. 39.
39. María Soledad Arteaga Lechuga [1996] IV S.J.F. 679.

The action of voidness of marriage does not only proceed before the existence of marriages celebrated between different people or spouses, but also when the spouses in both marriages are the same, because a correct interpretation of such precept must be in the sense that the existence of the first marriage at the moment of contracting the second, voids automatically this one, because it is inferred that it was contracted in bad faith, because it is undoubted that if it is celebrated between the same spouses it cannot be discussed their not knowing the celebration of their first marriage, and the duplicity of two marital links cannot be legally accepted, independently of which the reasons for this contract may have been.[40]

40. Armando Francisco Benassini Togno et al. [1996] III S.J.F. 577.

Chapter 2. Divorce

§1. Grounds

74. Historically speaking, in our law, divorce did not exist and that was due to the influence of the European codifications in our juridical system, through the Spanish law that ruled formally in Mexico through the Colonial Age, found during three centuries starting in 1521, date of the conquest of Mexico, and up to 1821, date of the definite independence.

Ever since then, although the Spanish codification continued to rule, the movement of codification started to appear throughout in every one of the new entities that formed the independent territory of the Republic. In many cases, the French codification of 1804 had to be taken as a model, especially in its civil aspect through *Code Napoleon.*

The following important movement had its roots in the harsh fight settled, from a political –and a military– point of view, between conservatives and liberals, in the decade of the sixties of the nineteenth century. Thus, in the year 1856, the Reformation Laws (*Leyes de Reforma*) were drawn up by liberals, and in 1917 it was decreed the Law of Family Relations (*Ley de Relaciones Familiares*), where it was plenty recognized the possibility of resolution of the marital link.

75. Nowadays, all of the Republic's codes foresee the possibility of divorce. Article 266 of the CCDF does not define it, but it states concretely that 'The divorce dissolves the marital link and it leaves the spouses in aptitude to contract another.' We have to recognize that in this aspect things have changed a great deal in Mexican society, since as of the official data, in 1970 there were three divorces every 100 marriages; forty one years later, in 2011, there were already sixteen divorces in every 100 marriages. The states with the greater rate in divorces are Baja California, Chihuahua, Aguascalientes and Yucatan; and the states with the lesser rate in divorces are Hidalgo, Guerrero, Tlaxcala and Oaxaca.

§2. Procedure

76. The simplest and fastest form that divorce can be obtained is known under the denomination of *divorce by mutual consent of an administrative type*. Our Code foresees the possibility that the marital link can be dissolved by the simple declaration of both spouses, as long as other requirements are fulfilled, that consists in the fact that both are of age, that they do not have children, and that they have ended the patrimony relationship.[41]

---

41. The new Art. 272 CCDF sets out:

> The administrative divorce proceeds when having passed a year or longer since the celebration of marriage, both spouses converge in divorcing, either of age, may have finished the conjugal society of goods, if they are married under that patrimonial regime, the spouse is not pregnant, they do not have offsprings in common, or having them, they are of age, and do not require

If this is the case, both spouses must show up personally before the judge of the Civil Registry presenting at once the marriage certificate and manifesting in a terminant and explicit form their will to divorce.

However, the judge of the Civil Registry will demand the identification of the spouses and will proceed to the settlement of a certificate in which will be stated this divorce request. Then, he/she will appoint the spouses to present themselves to ratify fifteen days later.[42] Once the ratification is effected, the judge settles the corresponding certificate and will draw the declaration of divorce. Next he/she must write down the former marriage certificate.

77. The second kind of divorce is a variant a little more complex than the former kind. It presupposes that the spouses wish to divorce, but the extremes foreseen to the administrative divorce are not reunited, that is, that they are not of age yet, or that they have children, or that they have not ended the conjugal patrimony relationship, etc. Thus, this is a form of *divorce by mutual consent of a judicial type*.

If the spouses are found in any of these cases, then they are obliged to present an agreement to the Court. This agreement must contain decisions about the following

---

> alimony from the spouse. The Judge of the Civil Registry, previous identification of the spouses, will settle an act that will testify the divorce request and will appoint these for them to ratify it after fifteen days. If the spouses do so, the judge will declare them divorced and will do the corresponding writing in that of the former marriage.
>
> If it is proven that the spouses do not fulfill with the supposed demanded, divorce thus obtained won't produce any effects, independently of the sanctions foreseen in-laws.

In Mexico City, as well in some few provincial civil codes, namely Coahuila, Colima, Guerrero, Hidalgo, Mexico, Puebla, Sinaloa, Tamaulipas, and Yucatan, the new reforms in this matter allow the so-named 'no fault divorce', or 'unilateral divorce', or 'express divorce' (*divorcio sin causa*), foresee in Arts 266 and 267 CCDF, for example.

The Art. 266 CCDF, reformed in October 2008, says that 'May be requested by one or both spouses if either of them claim before the court expressing its unwillingness to continue the marriage, without requiring pinpoint the cause for which it is requested, provided there at least one year has elapsed since the date thereof'.

The requirements are as follow: to present two witnesses; to present certified copy of the marriage certificate; being both of them senior citizens; not having any children (or, in the case of having them, that they are senior citizens and being absolutely clever); having dissolved the conjugal society; in its case, to manifest the absence of pregnancy in the female; and, of course, to present the identification of both of divorcing parts.

It has been necessary to modify several articles in CCDF to establish the procedure related to this express divorce. The provisional pertinent measures are regulated in detail (Art. 282) and when the divorce is not gotten with a new agreement, it will be dictated an inter-locutory sentence to decide the situation of the children or of the goods. One of the key reforms have consisted in proposing the suppression of the second meeting of ratification, so that now the spouses will be able to get divorced in just one meeting. The resolution which authorizes the divorce is unappealable (Art. 685*bis* CPCDF).

A law in Coahuila in 1999 and with important reforms in 2008, still established that the divorce could only be done by envisaged causes in law and fully demonstrated (Art. 362). Just five years later, in 2013, in this same state another new law plainly approved the divorce without cause (Arts 362 and 365 CCCOAH).

Finally, a new law in Tamaulipas authorizes the divorce procedure in notary venue (Arts 163.1 fr. IV and 163.2 Notarial Law).

42. In Jalisco the term is thirty natural days (Art. 405*bis*), as established by a reform in 2007.

points: Designation of the person who will have the guard and custody of the minors; the form of attending the necessities of the offspring to whom must be given child support; the house which will serve as home to each spouse and the offspring; the amount or percentage of alimony for the creditor spouse; the form to administrate the assets of the conjugal relationship and the right to visit the offspring (see Article 147 CCVER, for example. The new reforms to the CCDF repealed Articles 273 and 276 that regulated the case).

Once the application with the respective agreement has been presented, accompanied by a certified copy of the certificate of marriage and birth certificates of minor children, the judge will call the spouses and the Public Prosecutor to a meeting. At this meeting, the judge has the duty to encourage the interested parties to reach a conciliation, but if this objective is not reached, it must then be given process to review and approve of provisionally, in its case, every one of the points of the agreement, listening to the Public Prosecutor.

If the will of the spouses to get divorced firmly continues, the tribunal must appoint a second meeting and once again has the obligation to encourage conciliation. If it is not obtained, the tribunal will proceed immediately to dictate sentence, deciding definitely over the proposed agreement.

It can also happen that the Public Prosecutor is opposed to any special point of the agreement. In this case the spouses have the obligation to propose the necessary modifications; once this is done, the tribunal concedes in benefit of the spouses in order to manifest in three days what is most convenient to their interests.

Authorized in this case the dissolution of the link, and passing the relative term for its refutation, the tribunal requests a certified copy of it for its remission to the judge of the Civil Registry, as stated in Article 682 CPCDF.

It is important to state, finally, that both procedures, administrative as well as judicial, for the previous approval of the agreement, cannot in any case be requested until after a year of the celebration of marriage.[43] This way, the legislator ensures that it is not the result of a passing caprice or a thoughtless decision of both spouses. In spite of everything, the spouses who may have requested this divorce in any of its two variants, will be able to reconcile at any time as long as the procedure lasts, because the final intention of the legislator lies, as it can be seen, in the maintenance of the marital link wherever possible. Even more, supposing that this may be the case, but then the consent of the spouses may change again and they insist on their divorce, the law imposes another mandatory period of waiting for a year, this time counted from the reconciliation.

78. The third and last form of divorce foreseen in our legislation takes place, diversely, by the existence of a serious cause, and it does not suppose, of course, the agreement of both spouses. Consequently, it bears the name of *contentious divorce*.

---

43. The CC of Nuevo León has approved *protection directives* or *restriction orders* since 2012 in its Arts 323*bis* 2 et seq. They can be issued for thirty days period validity, and to hold up the probable aggressor as for as 500 metres from the assumed victim (cf. *infra*, n. 75).

The new Art. 272 CCDF insists in the term of a year (this requirement disappears now in the Art. 274 which was unnecessarily repeated). In general, Mexican laws demand, certainly, one year of marriage to be able to ask for the divorce, but Zacatecas law demands only six months (Art. 215).

Some provincial civil codes declare a closed catalogue as follows: duly proven adultery; a conceived child born during marriage with any other different person; the proposal of a spouse to prostitute the other; the incitation or the violence or crime; the conduct to corrupt the offspring, as well as the tolerance in its corruption; any incurable disease contagious or hereditary and the irreversible sexual impotence; any incurable mental disorder; the unjustified separation of the conjugal house for more than six months; the separation of the spouses for more than a year; the declaration of absence legally done, or the assumption of death; the extreme cruelty, or the threats or serious injuries; the unjustified denial of the spouses to fulfil his/her economical obligations; the slanderous accusation done by a spouse against the other, for a some sort of crime; to have committed a crime on purpose by one of the spouses; the pernicious alcoholism or the habit of gambling; to commit, a spouse against the other, or against the offspring, a crime on purpose; the conduct of family violence; the unjustified non-accomplishment of the determinations of the administrative or judicial authorities that may have been ordered, tending to correct the acts of family violence; the use of illicit substances that may produce psychotic effects; the use of methods of assisted fertilization, done without the consent of the spouse, and to refrain a spouse to the other, to perform an activity.[44]

In relation to the cause about the unjustified separation of the conjugal house for more than six months, it is necessary to clarify that a recent decision of the federal tribunals has stated that:

> When the spouses live at their parents', another relative's, or third persons' house, there is no actual conjugal domicile, understanding for this, a place where the spouses can live with own authority, in equal conditions and where the woman must have under her charge the direction and administration of home.[45]

Finally, it is appropriate to refer here to the CC of Tabasco (Article 272, fr. XVIII), Baja California Sur (Article 289 fr. III), Morelos (Article 199, fr. XVII [compare Article 175, fr. XVII, FCMOR]), and the FC of Michoacán (Article 261, fr. XX), which add as a divorce cause the fact that the woman uses methods of artificial human conception without the consent of the husband. Besides, the CC of Morelos also states change of sex – or the mere attempt – as a valid cause for divorce (Article 199, fr. XXI [compare Article 175, fr. XX, FCMOR]).

79. The *procedure* to demand this form of divorce is found in the provincial civil procedures codes, but in a different place than administrative type divorce, because it does not maintain a specific procedure, but instead it is an ordinary trial (juicio ordinario civil).

It is interesting to note here, by now, the urgent provisional measures which the judge is obliged to adopt once the contentious divorce request has been established:

44. Other CC that have incorporated this specific causal are the ones from Baja California Sur (Art. 289, fr. VII), Tamaulipas (Art. 244, fr. XV), and Veracruz (Art. 141, fr. XVIII).
45. Bulmaro Manjarrez Téllez [1997] VI S.J.F. 675.

one of the main obligations of the tribunal consists in solving the physical separation of the spouses, frequently as a preventive measure to avoid the commission of any harm. Another important obligation that must be solved in an urgent form refers to alimony, specially about warranties. The tribunal is also obliged to take the necessary measures to protect the assets that are eventually found in the marital relationship, to protect the woman who is pregnant, and to take care of children putting them under the care of a person who might be designated by the spouses themselves. In some cases, as we said (compare note 44), the tribunal can also dictate measures that may restrict the freedom of movement of either of the spouses, even to prevent acts of family violence.

All of these measures are reinforced, besides, with specific dispositions foreseen in the civil procedures code. Thus this legal body foresees the right of the spouse to request the judge of family matters for a separation, except in the cases of urgency, because then any judge can declare the separation in a provisional form, but he/she must refer immediately the diligences to the competent judge.

The procedure is so expeditious that the separation request can even be demanded in a verbal form, relating briefly the circumstances in which the act takes place. However, the judge has all kinds of faculties to solve in a discretional form the practice of the diligences that are necessary; once these are effected, without further delay, the judge will do whatever may be necessary.

In any case, the plaintiff has the obligation to present formal suit or accusation within a brief term starting from the resolution, in a form that the cause that completes the process may be formally ventilated.

Thus, if the respective suit is not presented, the effects of the separation cease immediately and the separated spouse must go back to the house.[46]

80. From all of this it can be seen, then, the fundamental importance which the legislator grants to problems concerning the family. In fact the law expressly clarifies that these kinds of problems are considered of public importance, because the family constitutes the 'base of the integration of society'. In this same legislative policy, it is written that the obligation of the judge of family affairs is to exhort at all times the spouses to obtain a resolution or conciliation.

But it is also proven that the absence of specific formalities in this matter would just tend to burden the procedure, as well as the obligation of the judge to replace the deficiency of the parts in their juridical settings.

In some cases, as it was seen before, it is even enough with the simple personal presence to expose the most urgent cases, with which authority is found anyway to provide that necessary to evacuate the suing. In the event that one of the parties asks for professional help, the tribunal demands the indispensable presence of a lawyer with a registered title and a professional document.

It is also necessary to ensure that proof can be offered of the most varied type 'with no more limitation than their not being contrary to morality or they are forbidden by law'. At this point, it is interesting to note specifically the collaboration of social workers, with a high technical level of academic grading that falls

46. In Zacatecas, all the audiences of family procedures are secret, as established by law (Art. 216 FCZAC).

expressly under disposition of tribunals to verify the truth of the discussed facts. These social workers must attend the hearing in order to present the corresponding information. They can be interrogated directly by the judge and by the parties as well.

Another special feature in controversies of family conflicts has to do with the speed of the procedures. It is known that civil trials are, ordinarily, slow due to the rigorous and formal proceedings to evacuate. Nevertheless, as for family trials, it is expressly prescribed that the hearing must be held within a brief period and it is even ordered that the sentence must be pronounced at the same moment of the hearing or within the following few days, granting the judge freedom of form in its expedition and even indicating the necessity to do so in a brief and concise form.

Finally, it is important to mention that the local government of Mexico City and of a large part of the federative entities has conceded in recent years a wide importance to the ventilation of these kinds of problems. This is seen through the implementation of a number of social aid programmes that centre their efficiency in the immediate attention of the complaints, even without professional assessment, through multiple tramitation booths in absolutely charge-free consultations.

§3. Effects

81. It has already been mentioned (*supra*, paragraph 75) that Article 266 CCDF establishes that in our country the definite dissolution of the marital link is completely accepted. Thus, the divorce leaves the spouses free to contract a new marriage. This disposition is repeated in the terms of Article 289 that does not have any more limitations. Nevertheless, the civil provincial codes limit this right in the case of the guilty spouse, because he/she will not be able to remarry until the term of two years has passed counted from the dissolution of the marital link. It is also important to state that even the divorced spouses in a voluntary form, cannot contract a marriage for a year after the divorce.

82. What happens in relation to children? Article 283 CCDF establishes that the sentence of divorce definitely fixes this situation, in all things concerning the effects of their physical custody and care.[47]

It has already been said that the Mexican laws establishes the public character of familiar conflicts because the family is 'the base of the integration of society'. Then,

47. The reform in 2007 in Mexico City has increased the age of children who will be guarded by the mother, since originally the limit was established at seven years; and now, in the cases of family violence, it can be increased up to twelve years (Art. 282, b, clause 2 *in fine*). It is the same case in the CCMEX, Art. 4.95, 2012, and CCNL Art. 414*bis*, 2012. In a reform in 2005, the Civil Code in Coahuila insists that children less than seven years of age have to be guarded by the mother (Art. 377, fr. V, CCCOAH. Cf. Art. 156, fr. VI, CCVER). By the way, the Code adds that in the case of children less than fourteen years old, it is the judge who will finally decide; the adolescents will be able to decide by themselves (Art. 552 CCCOAH).

Another reform, this time in 2003, authorizes the volunteer subrogation in the tenancy agreement of the house functioning as home to the couple. Thus, in case of divorce, the woman can stay with children in the mentioned house. The law also applies to concubinage (Art. 2448 CCDF).

on this same point, Article 282 B III remarks on the character of superior interest[48] which the care and protection of siblings has.

A principle that overcomes all the facts consists in the persistence of the obligations of parents towards siblings, even, in case of loss of parental custody (Article 285 CCDF). In this way, even divorced parents continue to have the obligation to contribute according to their earnings,[49] to the subsistence, education and necessities of siblings, up to the age of majority, or till 25 years of age, in the case of children following university courses, as we said before (e.g., Article 293 CCQRO).

83. Let us analyse now the effects of divorce in relation to assets. Once a definite sentence has been obtained, the judge orders to proceed to the division of the common goods. It has already been said in the case of divorce by mutual consent, in its two variants, that the problem must be solved from the beginning, precisely in the act of the request, that it is the respective agreement which is presented and discussed by both spouses, the social representation and the own judge during the process.

As for the contentious divorce, the question about the common goods makes it even more difficult to resolve a conflict which is complex in itself. Civil provincial codes set out, however, that one of the patrimonial consequences of divorce is to condemn the 'guilty spouse' to the loss of what he/she may have been granted or promised by the spouse and even by another person in consideration of the latter. As for the 'innocent spouse', he/she can keep all that he/she has received and even claim those benefits which may have already been arranged. As a result of new legal reforms, a spouse may request till 50% by concept of 'pecuniary compensation', just in the case he/she had worked domestically –at home – or taken care of children (e.g., Article 368 CCCOAH, 2013, and Article 268 CCQRO).

The division of goods presupposes the fulfilling of the pendant obligations between the spouses, and more widely, in the familial nucleus that includes the siblings. This division must also take into account the payment of the repairs that may have been mentioned in the sentence because of the consequential damages and loss of profits caused to the innocent spouse. Our law addresses that the guilty one must assume the responsibility in the terms of which the author of an illegitimate fact should assume it.

Finally, once divorce has been pronounced, the family judge is obliged to draw up a certified copy of the act and, naturally, to send it to the judge of the Civil Registry of the jurisdiction where the marriage may have taken place. This last functionary has the obligation to proceed to settle the corresponding statement, making the necessary entry in its precedent. The judge must, as well, publish an extract of the resolution on the Registry's bulletin board, which must be displayed for a few days.

---

48. At this point the law in Coahuila, reformed in 2005, it also expressly accepts the principle of 'superior interest of the minor' (Art. 21; cf. Art. 293 CCPUE, *supra* 6 and *infra* 108).
49. In this context the 2010 Civil Code reforms in Tamaulipas provide that when it is not verifiable salary, the judge will resolve based on the debtor's past two years 'standard of living'.

Chapter 3. Cohabitation without Marriage

84. We have already established (*supra*, paragraphs 61 and 80) that our civil legislation attaches very special importance to the marital institution. Proof of it resides in the complex solemnity of the requirements that must be observed in the celebration of the same act (Articles 97–113 CCDF) and in the incorporation of demands to ensure the establishment and stable development of family (Article 4 CPEUM; Articles 162–164, 168 CCDF; Article 940 CPCDF).

In the philosophical dogma of this context, precise attention should be paid to the obvious marginal importance that the legislator attaches to other kinds of institutions apart from the legal formality that the marital institution signifies. This is the case, precisely, in relations that are entered with people who are not married. Our civil legislation grants the qualifier of *concubinage* to what in the popular language is known as living together or cohabitation.

Nevertheless, from the social point of view this free union occurs quite frequently in present times, because of reasons of mutual conviction – and that derives then from a different form to conceive life –, or because of imposed reasons by social and economic reality nowadays. Therefore, the legislator has had to confront, in one way or the other, this social problem. As national statistics show, eight people out of ten are married, and the remaining two live in concubinage.

85. Little by little, civil and family legislations in the Republic are legally recognizing the possibility of the concubinage.[50] But, regardless of recognition of this situation, the legislator accepts however the legal regulation of *some* of its consequences (e.g., as it is stated in the Article 4.404 CCMEX).

The first and most frequent case is the recognition of *succession rights* that the spouses have between themselves. The analysis of this problem will take place in Part IV of this same essay, regarding the people who have the right to inherit (*infra*, paragraph 180).

Second, another important case of the regulation of consequences is produced in *alimony duty.* A large number of legislations, certainly, authorize the payment of alimony in the concubinage relationship.[51]

---

50. Just a few codes, the CC of the states of Baja California Sur (Art. 330), Mexico (Art. 4.403), Nuevo Leon (Art. 291*bis*), Puebla (Art. 297), and the FC of Hidalgo (Art. 146) and Zacatecas (Art. 241) contain a definition of concubinage. Herein is the latter definition: 'The concubinage is a marriage in fact; it is the union between a man and a woman free of marriage and with no impediments that law might appoint to celebrate it, that in a public and permanent form, do live in common, as if they were married, if such union lasts more than five years or they may procreate a son'.

    It is necessary to mention here that the FCHGO (Art. 150 fr. II) demands the inscription of the concubinage in the book of marriages of the Family State's Registry (*Registro del Estado Familiar*). By the way, the new reforms to the CCDF incorporate a whole chapter to this figure (Ch. XI: *Del concubinato*, Arts 291*bis*–291*quintus*).

51. Thus, the CC of the states of Baja California Sur and Guerrero and the FC of Hidalgo appoint the concubinage as a legal source of alimony duty. The CC from Tabasco and Tlaxcala, and the FC of Zacatecas establish in respect to this obligation, the equality between spouses and concubines.

    In some entities other requirements are established for the origin of alimony: The CCDF and the CCNL demand two years living together or having procreated children. The obligation is void if there are several concubines (the CC of Chihuahua, Sonora, Yucatán and the FCMICH coincide on

A third case takes place in the eventual protection that the law grants to the protection (*depósito*) of the person subject to some kind of *violence* or imminent danger in the intimate relationship of concubinage.

Fourthly, another supposition takes place when the Civil Code establishes *assumptions in relation to the children* born from this union. Thus, the Article 383 CCDF spreads out the legal assumption to recognize as children of the concubines the children who are born from the concubinage and to those born in the period of the 300 days following that, when this relation may have finished.[52]

As a matter of fact, the reforms in 2000 in Mexico City confirmed the fact that this relationship generates between the concubines *succession rights*, and food benefits, and are attributed all rights and obligations inherent to the family where they apply. Finally, to have the benefit of a food pension in a term equal to the duration of the concubinage (Articles 291*ter*, 291*quater* and 291*quintus* CCDF).

---

it). The FC of Zacatecas (Arts 241 and 242 fr. II) and Morelos (Art. 65) however, demand that the union last for more than five years. However, the CC of Chiapas appoints only three years of cohabitation, that the beneficiary has an honest way of living, and that both have remained as single. Besides, it specifies that if the male is handicapped and without resources for his subsistence, this will then at the same time become the woman's alimentary creditor.

The CC of Tamaulipas and Veracruz coincide that the cohabitation as a couple will be three years – or less if there are children – as long as they do not marry a third person. The CC of Queretaro, on the other hand, appoints that the alimony obligation arises during all the time that the concubinary relation may last and it may even last for a time equal to its endurance, once ended, as long as the creditor does not have another couple and lives honestly.

52. The 'constant possession of state of son' evidence supposes the proving of circumstances such as the child has been treated as son or daughter, or his or her has used the father's surname, or that the father has given him or her the elementary supplies.

As it is natural, the assumed father must have the minimal age to contract marriage, plus the son's age who is going to be recognized, but in the state of Guanajuato the law just asks for a eleven years difference between both of them, and even the CCDF (2004 reforms) does no longer demand this latter requirement.

Some codes establish expressedly the filiation of children born outside marriage, in relation to the mother, just for the single fact of the birth and they admit all the means of proof to justify such circumstance (Art. 346 CCTAB; Art. 322 CCZAC; Art. 393 CCBCS; Art. 195 CCTLAX; Art. 321 CCTAMPS).

It is necessary to mention that the CC of Tabasco (Art. 347) consignates in an expressed form the legal assumption of maternity in the event of artificial conception, in the following terms:

> when in the productive process a second mother participates, it will be assumed legal mother the one who contracts, either this last supplying the ovule or not. That is, when the substitute mother is not the biological mother of the child born as result of a transference of embryo, the contracting mother must be considered as the child's legal mother and this will be considered legitimate son of the woman who contracted.

As it is established by a reform in October 2007, the FCZAC examines the concept of *concubinage incomes*, that is to say, 'The incomes and benefits obtained with the common effort of the couple o concubines, in the administration of common goods or personal goods which serve to the home sustain, and offspring guard and education, and it does not matter that the property and possession of the mentioned goods is kept by the one having the right to it (Art. 139).' This community of *concubinage incomes* comes into effect from the very moment where the concubinage starts.

Chapter 4. Filiation

§1. Children Born in Wedlock

86. The word filiation comes from the Latin word *filius* that means son, and designates the special relationship between parents and children.

Inside wedlock, there are certain terms in virtue of which it must be assumed that a newborn child is the child of the spouses. This is the case, certainly, with babies who have been born after 180 days counted from the date of celebration of marriage and those children born into the following 300 days to the dissolution of the same.[53]

As is seen, in both cases the law establishes rigid cases of legal assumption in the protection of the newly born, in order to juridically cover adequately the real situations.

Now, both assumptions have their limits. For example, it is obvious that if the husband proves that he was physically unable to have maintained sexual relations with his spouse, such legal assumption cannot take place. For that effect, the Code accounts with 120 days of those first 300 that have preceded the birth.

There is another even more dramatic case. Let us suppose now that the spouse and mother of the baby confesses that the child is not the child from the husband and, therefore, admits an adulterous relationship. Then, not even in this case can the husband not recognize the children.

It is obvious that great care has been taken regarding the juridical protection of minors, taking into consideration the important task of the legislator. As with all rules, there are true exceptions, as well in this case: that the baby's birth has been hidden from the father, or that he proves that during the former ten months he could not have had sexual relations with his spouse.[54]

87. There are other assumptions of the same kind. As it has been stated in terms set out in Article 324 fr. I CCDF, the husband must recognize that he is the father of the child born of the marriage. In this case, there is not only a legal assumption, but it is also impossible to refute it. For example, if the husband knew about the pregnancy before getting married (a written proof is requested); it is the same case if he was present at the act of registration of the baby or if he expressly recognized him. A last cause resides in the lack of life viability, that is, that the child may not have been capable to live.

Article 328 CCDF is now repealed, but it continues in force in provincial codes (e.g., Article 259 CCVER).

---

53. Article 324 CCDF does not grant more a term of 180 days. The new article just reads as follows: 'It is presumed as offsprings of the spouses, except with proof against it: I. The offsprings born inside marriage ... '
54. There are a few differences in the codes of the federative entities. Thus, the CC of the State of Guerrero (Art. 501) only states the first supposition, that is, the one that refers to the hiding of the birth. Diversely, the CC of Chihuahua (Art. 303) and Morelos (Art. 208 [cf. Art. 183 CFMOR]) add the 'physical impossibility to engender'. Finally, the CC of Yucatan and Baja California Sur do not contain any provision with regard to this.

88. The *terms of prescription* are different as well. The general rule is that the husband has a term of sixty days counting from the day that he learns of the birth of the baby to refute the filiation (Article 330 CCDF). However, it may happen that the husband does not know the date of birth, for example, in the case of absence. In this case, the term begins to run from the date of his return. Finally, it may happen that the baby's birth may have been hidden deliberately from him, in which case it is obvious that the sixty-day term can begin from the date on which the husband discovers the deception (Article 261 CCVER).

An exception to this general rule is concerning to the child who is born outside the term of 300 days after the dissolution of marriage, because in this hypothesis the father can argue the paternity at all times.

89. What happens in the case where the husband is either legally or physically disabled? At this supposition, the husband should be placed under guardian protection and, according to Article 449 of the CCDF, the guardian is obligated to promote the corresponding action. If this does not happen, once the husband becomes capable, he must promote the action. The term must be counted starting from the day when the ceasing of incapacity is judicially decreed, which evidently elongates the term that the husband has for its exercise, in terms of the time that must be invested to follow the suit.

In this same supposition, things may be even more complicated. Let us suppose, certainly, that the incapable spouse dies in those circumstances. The Code considers it fair that the heirs maintain the titularity of the action to contradict the questioned paternity. However, this rule also has an exception: The heirs cannot refute the paternity of the child born within the marriage, if the spouse did not manifest judicial interest on filing of a complaint.

90. There are other legal assumptions that have to do with the case of remarriage of a widow, divorcee or of those whose marriage may have been void. It is already known that in this case the former Article 158 CCDF now revoked, forbade the woman to marry again within a term less than 300 days. But this prohibition could be violated and, if so, what would the child's situation be? Article 334 now revoked too – but only in Mexico City –, resolved the situation assuming that the child is of the first marriage if he or she is born within 300 days after the dissolution of the first marriage and before 180 days from the celebration of the second; assuming, too, that the offspring is of the second husband if he or she is born after 180 days from the celebration of the second marriage, although the birth takes place within the 300 days after the dissolution of the first marriage; assuming, finally, that the child is born out of wedlock if the baby is born 180 days before the celebration of the second marriage and after 300 days of the dissolution of the first.

91. Let us now focus the matter relative to the case of *contesting paternity*. As it is obvious, the case where the corresponding suit in the judicial trial must be settled and the mother and her own child whose filiation is refuted must certainly be convoked to trial. As for the case in which the child were older than 18, it is evident that he will be able to show up for himself; if this were not the situation, a temporary guardian must be provided.

The trial must be followed in the ordinary form and according to that stated in the CPCDF. In all controversy that must be seen over filiation, according to these dispositions, there is no form of transaction. The negotiation for the arbitral opinion can also not be compromised. Then, this maxim produces an exception that deserves to be mentioned: regarding facts that the law has qualified of superior interest as to minors, the necessity of the former measure is understood. However, it can also result in collateral economic facts with respect to those transactions that can take place. In that case, such economical arrangements cannot presume at any time the recognition over the state of the child of the marriage.

The ordinary form of proving the filiation is, of course, the birth, settled precisely in the terms that we have already stated (*supra*, paragraph 24).

Now, it may be that the birth certificate does not exist, or it is even defective, incomplete or false. If this is so, the Code prescribes the utilization of a fact technicality that consists in the 'constant possession of state of son' (Article 341 CCDF; compare note 55).

In an extreme situation, it may be that even the proof of this situation could be rather difficult. If this is so, the law authorizes any other means of convincing proof, except the testimonial, because in this case the proof must be reinforced and administered with some other presumptive evidence that may produce conviction with the judge.

It is also certain that other circumstances may appear which certainly aid the case, for instance, where a child may have used the father's surname – the assumed father – without any opposition and even with his consent, or that this last may have always considered him as such, for external facts. Finally, it is obvious that any of these circumstances must be consistent with the difference of age that results from the descendent.

§2. Children Born Out of Wedlock

92. The relationship of children towards the mother is, for natural reasons, unquestionable from the legal point of view. As the law says, it results 'from the single fact of birth' (*mater semper certa est*).[55] The question, however, appears much more complex in the case of the father. For such effect, the law recognizes just two situations: the first one appeals directly to the expressed and spontaneous recognition by the father in respect of the child; the second has to do, diversely, with the obligatory compulsion before a tribunal.

93. As it has been said, the first situation is the simplest. In this case anybody can recognize a child if he has the required age to contract marriage, plus the age

55. Nevertheless, the new Art. 360 CCDF does not mention more this legal maxim.

of whoever is going to be recognized.[56] However the unborn child yet, can also be recognized.[57]

The act of recognition is exclusively individual and has absolutely no bias in respect of the other parent. It also has another characteristic: It is irrevocable and, therefore, it cannot be contradicted even when as in the case of a will, the testamentary disposition has been prepared and that act is cancelled later. Certainly, the Code maintains an expressed disposition in the sense that, even if the testamentary disposition is cancelled, the recognition persist on the same terms.

Let us now examine what happens when a minor has procreated a baby. In this hypothesis, the minor must ask for parents' permission in order to be able to recognize his/her child (Article 362, CCDF). Such recognition, carried out by the minor, can be questionable, precisely in view of his/her lack of capacity. Thus, a minor can easily be deceived by the assumed paternity. If it is proven that the paternity results are false or the minor himself/herself can refute such recognition once he reaches the age of 18. In this case he has a term of four years to try the corresponding action.

What is the procedure for recognizing a child born out of wedlock? The first and the most direct path is, of course, to go before the judge of the Civil Registry and request the settlement of the applicable birth certificate. The judge is obliged to carry out the relative transaction in the usual form. The second possibility lies in settling a special certificate before the same functionary. In this case the matter falls under the supposition set out in Articles 78–83 CCDF and the judge settles a certificate of recognition, writing down the original birth certificate. In the third place, the recognition of the child can be done in a public act before a notary public. Thus, the notary must proceed to the settlement of the document observing the formalities demanded in the Notarial Law and stating in a clear and expressed form the spontaneous and free recognition of paternity and establishing, undoubtedly, the identification of parent to child.

94. Finally, the recognition of the child can also be done in a judicial venue. In this last hypothesis two variants can be adopted, as there may be an ordinary procedure, or one must be settled in a voluntary special procedure. In the first case, ordinary procedure, it may happen that having started any legal action, the assumed parent shows up before the judge and at some period of time during the process confesses, in a direct and expressed form, that he is the father of the minor. In the second case, voluntary special procedure, the person shows up by means of an expressed request before a civil judge without litigation case, and recognizes the paternity.

---

56. As we have already mentioned (*supra,* para. 85, n. 52), the reform in Mexico City demands only the age enough to get married, eliminating the phrase 'plus the age of the child who is going to be recognized' (Art. 361 CCDF).
57. Articles 364–365 CCDF are now derogated. Their text was:

    Article. 364. It may be recognized the child who has not been born yet, as well as the one who has already died if he has left descendants.

    Article. 365. Parents may recognize their offspring, together, or separately.

It has already been said that the recognition of a son only takes effect in an exclusive form in respect to the parent requesting, and not in respect to the other parent. So, judges of the Civil Registry as well as notaries and judicial functionaries are strictly forbidden to make any investigation regarding the paternity of the remaining parent. Even functionaries must delete any revelation that may give them some knowledge of that person. Sanctions are severe because they consist in the destitution of the employment and in the inability to carry out another governmental one.

95. Two different hypothesis of recognition have already been analysed from the parent's point of view, that is, when this fulfils the required minimum age or else, in a different hypothesis, when it concerns a minor. Let us now look at the situation from the opposite extreme, that is, when the person who is to be recognized is of age. In this case, it seems quite clear that the child's consent must be obtained and, certainly, it is prescribed in Article 375 CCDF.

Let us now suppose on the other hand, that the person who will be recognized is a minor. If he/she has a guardian, his/her consent must be obtained; if he/she does not have one, the judge must name a guardian and we have already stated that this guardian carries the denomination of 'temporary'. In any case, the minor recognized has the action of refutation in his/her favour, once he/she obtained the age of majority. However, diversely to that stated in Article 363 – for whose hypothesis four years are granted – in this case only a two-year term is granted for the exercise of the corresponding action.

What is the reason for this divergence? It seems clear that the legislator has considered the act of recognition of the child done by the minor, worthy of major judicial protection than the act of being recognized.

96. It is necessary to analyse now a series of hypothesis that refer diversely to the physical custody of the child recognized. The first question that comes up has to do with the parents who live separately, because it logically displays the problem that once recognition has been performed, by one or by both, of who should care for the minor. If both parents, even without living together, recognize voluntarily the minor, it is necessary to expect that they reach agreement in respect of who must take care of the child recognized. If this is not so, the matter must take a judicial form and be presented then to the judge, listening to the parents and the Public Prosecutor, to solve the problem.

97. Let us examine now the second question, that is, the case of parents who do not live together and who recognize voluntarily the minor, but not simultaneously. With regard to the phrase (which seems frivolous in this case) of *prior tempore, potior iure*, it is clear that whoever recognized the minor first, must then have preference in the exercise of custody. In any case, it is important to always remember that there should be free negotiation about the settlement of custody between the parents. Finally, in case of disagreement, the matter must be solved according to previous criterion, that is, judicial intervention with the opinion of the Public Prosecutor.

However, there may appear different circumstances which complicate the matter. Let us suppose now the case of the nanny or baby sitter[58] who has been taking care of a baby. It is obvious that by having assumed this responsibility in a voluntary way, the woman has generated a duty of care and with it, certain rights over the minor. So, in certain cases, a judicial decree may permit her not to be separated from the mentioned minor. However, the woman must then proceed to contradict the recognition on a firm basis. She has sixty days to do so.

98. Many cases will not be able, however, to be solved through free and spontaneous recognition. Then there is no other resource but to proceed to investigate, via the means available, the corresponding paternity. The Code indicated that this investigation was allowed only in some expressly determined cases. They were reduced to the events of a kidnapping, violation, or rape, when the time of the crime coincides with the one of the conception; when the child is found in 'constant possession of state of son' of the assumed father; when the child has been conceived during the time when the mother was living under the same roof with the assumed father in a marital way; and when the child has in his or her favour a presumptive evidence against the assumed father (Article 382 CCDF, now repealed[59]).

99. Who can investigate paternity? Of course, it can be done by the child born out of wedlock and even by his descendants. However, it is important that the investigation must be carried out precisely during the life of assumed parents. When the descendant is already of age, and has legal capacity for the exercise of judicial actions, no problem at all is grounded. But, what if he/she is a minor or an incapable person? It has already been said previously that this action can be tried through the local representatives; even the Code grants an exception elongating the time of investigation to the four years immediately after reaching the age of majority.

In a contrary sense, the investigation of maternity is not allowed when the responsibility is given to a married woman, except if there is a civil or criminal sentence.

Any other ordinary means of proof is admissible in the investigation, because the reforms in 2000 in Mexico City state now that paternity and maternity can be proved by biological means. If the presumed progenitor denies to give the biological sample, they are presumed to be the parents, excepted if it is proven the opposite (Article 382).[60] The simple fact of giving child support is not a true proof of paternity or maternity. There is not even an assumption and it cannot function as a basis to start the corresponding investigation. Finally, once recognized, and even being outside marriage, the child has the following rights: to use his parents' surname, to be fed, right to hereditary succession and any other rights as a consequence from the act of filiation (Article 389 CCDF).

---

58. Now it is possible, in terms of the new Art. 378 CCDF, that the baby sitter may not only be a female, but a male.
59. This Art. 382 was recently derogated, but only in the CCDF. It continues in force in provincial codes. The new – absolutely new – Art. 382 does not say anything in this respect.
60. This is for example, in provincial codes, the cases of CCJAL, 2007, Art. 491, para. 2nd; CCVER, 2010, Art. 314, fr. IV; CCHGO, 2010, Art. 804 *in fine*; and Nuevo Leon since 2012, Art. 381*bis*, with DNA evidences.

100. In relation to filiation, a last institution acquainted under the name of *legitimacy* is recognized. This is a benevolent institution, of exceptional features, that establishes a fiction of legal nature. Thus the latter marriage that is verified between parents produces the effect of considering children in such union, to be born *in* wedlock. In this form, the Code has legitimated the children who would be formerly considered only as *natural children*. The process to effectuate such legitimacy consists in the parents' expressed recognition of the son before marriage or at the same moment of its celebration, or even during the conjugal relationship.

As a consequence of this phenomenon of legitimacy, the rights of children, that are plainly defined, must claim to be retroactive to the precise moment of the celebration of marriage. This legal fiction is so wide that even in the event that the son may have died, he can still obtain the legitimacy in order to legitimate his descendants, that is, the spouse's grandchildren.

Finally, the son who is expected can be recognized in the act of marriage, if the woman is, at that time, pregnant.

It is important to note here that the chapter dedicated to legitimacy was absolutely revoked in the CCDF (Articles 354–359) in 2000 reform process, but this is not the case of the new FCSIN (Articles 257–260), 2013.

Chapter 5. Adoption

101. The word adoption comes from the Latin words *ad* and *optare*, that expresses the idea of wishing or wanting something, in this case to look for the protection and care of the minor or incapacitated person. The adoption, thus, must be beneficial for the adopted person. At this point, the legal normative repeats the same concept as in other parts that the most important consideration to take into account has presided, that is, the *superior interest* of the minors or physically or intellectually challenged adults. It cannot be possible to adopt an adult, except physically challenged, as we already said, but a new law in the state of Aguascalientes, 2010, it makes this new hypothesis possible (Article 413, V, *in fine*).

As it has been seen, the law establishes a series of requirements which the person who wants to adopt must fulfil. In the CCDF the following requirements are established for the adoption: The person who desires to adopt must be older than 25 years of age;[61] to be free of marriage; to have the free exercise of his or her rights; to be 16 years older than the adopted;[62] to have enough economical assets; and to be in an ideal situation to develop the adoptive function in an adequate form. Article 390 refers to person remaining as free of marriage. This is the general rule. It may seem strange, undoubtedly, that the requirement defined bachelorhood and not in the marital institution. In Article 392 the rule is expressly repeated: 'no one can be adopted for more than a person ...'

What reasons could the legislator have had? The fundamental argument lies in the fact of not throwing into the institutional life of marriage an element of strange consideration that of course is produced with the incorporation of a minor or physically or mentally challenged. From this point of view, the legislator has preferred to transfer that responsibility to a single person and even in this irregular situation to trust that the minor would be duly protected. In any case, it does not prevent the pretension of locating a father and a mother for the unprotected minor or handicapped. In conclusion, the legislator has decided to choose the least bad option among the few alternatives that it had in the case.

However, that is not an obstacle for, in the opposite extreme, the person who was considered as an ideal adoptant, could then adopt one or more persons, even in a simultaneous form if peculiar circumstances come together.

Nevertheless, there is an important case of exception. The spouses or concubines can adopt, but as long as both conform conscientiously to the seriousness of the situation. That is the case foreseen as an exceptional hypothesis in Article 391 CCDF, but it is not the novelty case of the state of Queretaro, where either of both spouses – or both concubines – have a preference right to adoption as compared to single persons (Article 380 CCQRO).

102. The requirements that the adoptant must fulfil have already been mentioned. Let us examine now what happens with the adopted person. If the adopted

---

61. In Morelos the adoptant has to be of twenty-eight years of age (Art. 361, reforms 2007).
62. In Aguascalientes (Art. 413) and Jalisco (Art. 543) must to be fifteen years old, and of twenty-five years old in Veracruz (Art. 320), but all these differences in years are legally irrelevant in the case of intellectual or physically or incapable non-minority persons.

person is older than 12 years, the Code considers fair that he or she be asked for consent. In any case, if the person to be adopted were under the age of 12 years or absolutely incapable – whatever his or her age may be – the Code demands the consent of the persons who, in any form, have the legal representation. Thus, the consent in the adoption of whoever exercises the parental custody, the tutor, who has the simple custody, the Public Prosecutor, and the assistance institutions that may have eventually taken care of the minor, must always be sought.

It may happen that any of these individuals may oppose the adoption. If this is the case, the reason must be stated clearly, and the matter must then be given to the competence of the corresponding judge, who must then proceed to the qualification of the motive, always taking into consideration, of course, the superior interest that we have already made reference to. Now, due to reforms in Mexico City, it is possible to adopt a totally capable adult (Article 393, III, CCDF).

103. The *procedure* to effectuate an adoption is regulated in Articles 923–925 CPCDF. Of course, there must be a presentation of the documents that credit the facts foreseen by Article 397 CCDF. In this initial presentation the other data that might be essential must also be presented; that is, name and age of the physically challenged minor and of the people who show up as his/her representatives, either under the form of parental custody, tutorship or altruistic representation. The judge will receive immediately the presentation accompanied by pertinent proof and will take provisions to decree the placing of the minor or physically challenged, precisely with the assumed adoptant, for a term of six months.

Next, the judge must proceed to bring together the consent of the persons who must give it, according to that stated in the CCDF. By the third day the judge must definitely render his/her judgment without further delay.

As has been seen, the procedure gives very expeditious results and disregards all other formalities that may be cause for delay. In this way the interests of the minor or physically challenged who might eventually be found in a situation of trouble or need, are duly protected.

The procedure is similar in the inverse sense, that is, in case of revoking, because the intervention of the judge is reduced to effectuate appointments for verbal audience, where he/she must immediately solve the convenience of the revoking. Of course, the opinion of the same persons who initially gave their consent must be heard again. As in other similar cases, all kinds of proof that the judge may take into consideration can be produced.

Finally, the case of refutation is different, both regarding adoption, as its revoking, because in this case such procedures can by no means be promoted in voluntary trial.

104. It has already been mentioned before that not so long ago our codes did not recognize the plain or total adoption. Starting from recent reformations, this term has been incorporated into our civil law. The term of the simple adoption that already existed has been however conserved in some provincial codes. Thus, regarding this variant, the relation that arises from the adoption established legally between adoptant and adopted can be revoked.

105. This revoking can take place, in the most obvious case, when both parties consent to it and the latter supposes, of course, the consent of the adopted. If it were not so, then the consent of those who exercise the parental custody, tutor, guardian, Public Prosecutor or government institutions of assistance that may have intervened in the case, must be obtained.

Another expressed case that the law deals is the ingratitude of the adopted. This involves a concept of sentimental character that, however, reaches noticeable juridical relevance in some specific cases, for instance, in donations and in this particular case of adoption.

Fortunately, the provincial civil codes define undoubtedly the concept of ingratitude in the specific circumstances that may take place. The ingratitude of the adopted is considered in the following cases:

(i) if he or she commits any intentional crime against the person, the honour or the goods of the adoptant, of his/her spouse, of his or her ascendants or descendants;
(ii) if the adopted formulates a suing or trial against the adoptant, for any crime although proven, unless it had been committed against the adopted, his/her spouse, ascendants or descendants; and
(iii) if the adopted refuses to feed the adoptant who has fallen into poverty. (Article 336 CCVER, for example.)

Finally, another cause is characterized by the existence of serious danger for the minor.

It is a characteristic of the adoption in its simple variant that, once revoked, everything is restored precisely to the previous situation they were in before the adoption took place and thoroughly seems to form, of course, the peculiar nature of this adoption modality. Whatever it may be, it clearly results that, during the period in which the term of simple adoption takes place, the adopted has, towards the person who may adopt him, the same rights and obligations that a son may have, and vice versa, the one who adopts has, to in favour him, the same rights and obligations that as parents have. In any case, it must be recalled here that some special circumstance may occur, in the event of the simple adoption, therefore it is convenient not to transfer the names and surnames of the adoptant to the adopted person.

106. On the other hand, in our country a strong movement to recognize the plain – or total – adoption (*adopción plena*) has taken place, because most of our civil codes would only recognize simple adoption.[63]

Thus, let us now deal with the plain or total adoption. According to the modern tendencies that have been imposed on the affair, the adopted must be compared in

63. The CC of the states of Jalisco (Arts 533 and 539), Guerrero (Arts 561 and 571), Quintana Roo (Arts 929 and 939), Guanajuato (Arts 456 and 460), Tabasco (Arts 381 and 398) and Baja California Sur (Arts 428 and 438) still classify the adoption in its modalities of *simple* and *plain*. Yucatan suffered a reform in 2005 which is still effective (Art. 309 A).

On the other hand, the FC from Zacatecas (Art. 355), Hidalgo (Art. 216), Michoacan (Art. 382), and Sinaloa (Art. 390), and the CCDF (Art. 328) just consignate the plain adoption. The CC of Nuevo Leon (Art. 402) and Coahuila (Art. 501) name *semiplain* to the *simple* adoption.

all legal effects to the son related by blood. It is clear that, under these circumstances, both adoptant and adopted will have exactly the same rights and obligations as are established in a correlative form in that supposition and the adopted assumes then, also, the surname of whoever adopts him.

A rather remarkable situation has to do with the extinction of the former filiation, that is, with the previous state of the child who up to that point would maintain the adopted with his natural parents, making all legal and natural links with the former family unavailable.

In the seriousness of that context and in the new legal situation that consequently emerges, it must be seriously considered that this sort of adoption is essentially irrevocable and, therefore, there is no room for the consideration of elements of sentimental ordeal, such as ingratitude or the decision to alter the consent, even founded in objective causes.

In the state of Sinaloa is mandatory to have a familiar custody before the definitive adoption must have place (Article 336 FCSIN).

As it was exposed in the former case, the adoption must be consented to by the concerned people and authorities, those who exercise the parental authority, the tutor, the Public Prosecutor, and by the minor if he is older than 12, because in all matters of adoption the minors will be heard depending on their respective ages and degree of maturity. Also, the family who may have hosted the minor and treats him as a son or daughter, will be able to oppose the adoption, having to explain the reasons.

Now, if those who exercise the parental authority are at the same time subjected to it, the subject's parents will have to consent in the adoption if they are present; otherwise, the judge of family affairs will provide the consent.

In all of this there are only two limitations: first, the consideration of circumstances that may refrain marriage, according to that stated in Article 156 CCDF. Thus, although the adoption extinguishes the pre-existent filiation, the biological relationship subsists. This consideration is reaffirmed with that set out in Article 406, fr. I, that obliges the registrar to refrain from supplying information, except in the precise case of finding out precedents to know the impediments to an eventual marriage.[64] Second, when the own adopted person decides to know about his or her family background (Article 406, II).

The CC of Jalisco (Art. 554), Federal District (Art. 410 E), and Baja California Sur (Art. 446), and the CF of Michoacan (Art. 386) and Morelos (Art. 371), foresee besides the modality of *international* adoption, promoted by foreign citizens with habitual residence outside the national territory; the adoption *by foreigners*, in exchange, is the one promoted by citizens from another country, but with permanent residence in the national territory.

By the way, it is interesting to see that the FC of Hidalgo and Zacatecas, and the CC from Oaxaca define the adoption as a *juridical act* (Arts 213, 351 and 403, respectively), while the CC from Jalisco states that it is a *juridical state* (Art. 520) and the CC from Guerrero precises its nature under the form of legal *institution* (Art. 554).

64. According to amendments in Mexico City, the adopted child is now compared to the blood son, which makes possible to apply marriage impediments. On the same way, the adoption eliminates the affiliation and the kinship existing previously, except precisely when it refers to the marriage impediments (cf. Arts 293, 295, 390 and 395, II, IV CCDF, 2011). In the same sense, cf. Arts 4.120 CCMEX, 2012 and 196 and 199 FCSIN, 2013. To the contrary, in other states the adoption remains as a civil kinship (e.g., Art. 413 CCAGS, 2010).

107. Finally, it is interesting to make here a brief reference to the *international adoption*. It is known that, certainly, during recent years many problems have arisen in relation to the transborder robbery of babies that were taken abroad in order to be picked up, obtaining thus good profits from people with no scruples. Thus, worried about the regulation of a situation that was already extremely alarming, our country included Articles 410 E and 410 F CCDF defining the concept of international adoption, its specific object and its legal regulation, that in this case is founded in the international treaties subscribed and ratified by the Mexican government.

Our Code distinguishes two types of international adoption. One refers to the international adoption thoroughly, promoted by foreign citizens but whose habitual residence is found outside the national territory. This is ruled by the international treaties already mentioned. The other one demands the permanent residence in Mexican territory and is solely ruled by the dispositions of the Civil Code.

Obviously, given the nature of this type of adoption, the international adoption is always plain. In equal conditions, the Mexican Republic state grants, of course, preference to citizens of the country before foreigners.[65]

65. In 2004 it has been reformed again the Art. 410 E. The modification consisted in adding the principle of bilateralism to the application of the international agreements and the elimination of the legend 'the international adoptions will always be full adoptions', not necessary, of course, in the new legal context.

Chapter 6. Parental Authority

108. The expression *patria potestad* comes from the Latin words *pater* and *potestas*, that refer to the elder authority of the head of the family in antique Rome. An authority that, as we all know, would maintain frequently powers of life or death over his subordinates.

Nowadays, the institution of parental authority is to a large extent regulated by the Civil Code. This regulation spreads out to the effects of the figure in the person and goods of the sons, and the suspension, loss and termination of the parental authority.[66]

According to the reforms in 2007 which refers to the convenience of the shared custody, the new text (Articles 411 and 414*bis* CCDF) emphasizes on the 'harmonic relationship' between the father and the sons 'regardless if they live or not in the same home'. It remarks the formula 'upbringing obligations'. These obligations are to give physical, psychological and sexual security; to promote adequate habits on food, personal hygiene and physical development; as well as promoting skills in intellectual and scholar development; to make affective demonstrations, with respect and acceptation of these ones by the child; and determine the limits and rules of behaviour preserving the superior interest of the minor.

These obligations exist even in the case of separation, because the right of coexistence with the child must always be kept (Articles 416, 416*bis* and 417).

Finally, the Article 416*ter* also reformed in 2007, defines which is denominated as 'superior interest of the minor' (compare *supra* 82) stating that it must be understood by this term the priority which has to be given to the rights of minors in front of the rights of any other person, in order to guarantee, among any others, the access to physical and mental health, food and education; to establish an environment of respect, acceptation and affection, free of any sort of family violence; the development of the personality structure, with an adequate self-esteem, free of overprotection and punitive excesses; the promotion of the personal and social responsibility; and other applicable legal rights.

109. The first question that arises about parental authority lies, certainly, in the subjects that exercise it. According to that set out in Article 414 CCDF, this faculty is exercised by parents. In the case that one of them dies, the remaining parent will continue to exercise authority. Now, if both parents die, the normative foresees that the exercise of the parental authority falls to the ascendants in second degree, that

66. Most of the codes in the Mexican Republic do not define parental authority. The CC of the states of Jalisco (Art. 578), Puebla (Art. 597), Baja California Sur (Art. 474) and the FCHGO (Art. 232) and FCSIN (Art. 347) do precisely define that concept. For example:

> The parental authority is a group of rights and obligations recognized and granted by law, to parents and grandparents in relation to their children or grandchildren, to take care of them, to protect them, and to bring them up, as well as his goods (CFHGO).

> Parental authority is a group of duties and obligations that reciprocally have, on one side the father and the mother, and on the other the children minors not emancipated, and whose objective is the guarding of the person and the goods of these minors, as well as their education' (CCPUE). The CC of Jalisco and Baja California Sur consignates this same last definition.

is, grandparents, and it must be clarified that at this point the law makes no distinction at all.[67] Thus, in the event of controversy, it is the judge of family who, taking into consideration the circumstances of the case, will resolve the conflict.[68]

The general principle that the institution of parental authority presides is, as Article 411 says, the mutual respect and consideration that must exist among ascendants and descendants, apart from their state, age and condition.[69]

110. The first right that arises from parental authority is the *right of shelter*. This way, those who exercise the parental authority always keep, on their side, the right to shelter their descendants, except of course, in the case where there is some kind of inconvenience for children. The goodness of this disposition may be appreciated even in the fact that the ascendants do not have the physical custody.

Thus, Article 416*bis* CCDF insists that the personal relations must be kept, as long as is fair, between the minor and his/her parents and that:

> Only through judicial commandment can be limited, or suspended the right to shelter that is referred to in the former paragraph, as well as in the cases of suspension or loss of parental authority, according to the modalities that for its exercise are established in the agreement or judicial resolution.

By other hand, Article 421 foresees that 'As the son were in the parental authority, he will not be able to leave the home of whoever exercises it without their permission or decree of the competent authority.' This disposition, however, is carefully reinforced in the practice by the insisting surveillance of the Foreign Relations' Secretary and of the notaries of all the Mexican Republic to demand at all times the reliable identification of the ascendants and the expressed ratified permission before the attestation of a notary.

111. The second important duty that an ascendant retains is the *right to surveillance*. This right is found foreseen as well in Article 418 and includes, of course, the faculty to correct the minor's behaviour.

The Proposal of Law of the Family for the State of Nuevo León (2007) created the need of parents' permissions for the control and surveillance of adolescents and young people in discotheques, bars and pubs. Similarly, the Proposal ordered the legal supervision of mass media advertisements and publicity (Article 27). In counterpart, the Code mentioned the obligation of the parents to observe such a behaviour that at all times serves as an example to the descendants.[70]

---

67. Except in the case of FCSIN, whose Arts 347 and 350 give a preference to the *maternal* grandfathers.
68. The new reforms in Mexico City (2007) and Michoacán (2008) now prevent the guarding and custody shared (Arts 282, B, II and 283*bis*, and 423 to 428, respectively), and the FCSIN (2013) states again that while juridically decided, the parental authority will be provisionally awarded to the *maternal* grandparents (Art. 353).
69. Other codes, for example the codes of Quintana Roo (Art. 991) and Tamaulipas (Art. 380), foresee the obligation only in an unilateral sense, determining that children must honour and respect their parents –without mentioning the inverse consideration.
70. The Proposal was finally rejected in the local Congress.

An innovative point in this subject is the creation of the 'schools for parents', commanded in the Law for the Family Protection of the State of Yucatan (Articles 15 and 16) and under the administration of the Department of Education. These schools for parents will have as a main goal to provide the elements to reinforce the relationships of living and the transmission of values, knowledge, skills, and attitudes towards the improvement of family (Article 15).

This faculty of surveillance and even to correct does not imply, of course, the use of violence or corporal punishment, that is forbidden by the reformation of Articles 323*ter*, 323*quater*, 323*quintus* and 323*sextus* CCDF which refer to family violence.[71,72] The reforms in 2007 to the new Article 323*quater*, fr. IV, second paragraph, insist on not to justify in any case the violence towards minors as a means of education.

71. However, the CC of the state of Guerrero does consignate expressly the right to punish ('measuredly') the minor, although it states that it does not imply hitting or mistreating him (Art. 589).
    New reforms in Tamaulipas and Coahuila foresee the fact that while divorce is not decreted, the spouses must avoid any act of manipulation aimed to produce resentment or alienation from child over the other progenitor (Arts 259*bis*, CCTAMP, 2010, and 554 CCCOAH, 2013).
72. On the other hand, the CC of Veracruz (Art. 254*bis*) is shown as one of the most advanced legislations on this point, because it contains an specific part related to the right that individuals have, as members of a family with respect to their physical and psychic integrity.
    In civil codes of Guerrero and Veracruz the prohibition of conduct that may generate *family violence* is defined as follows: 'the use of the physical or moral strength, as well as the serious omissions, that a member of the family may exercise against another member of the same, who attempts against his physical integrity, psychic integrity, or both, independently that it may produce or not injuries, as long as the aggressor and the attacked live at the same domicile and there is a relation of matrimony or concubinage'.
    In turn, reforms in 2007 in Mexico City classify now the forms of family violence in physical, psycho-emotional, economical, and sexual violence (Art. 323*quater*). The civil codes of the State of Mexico (Art. 4.397, in 2007), Puebla (Art. 291, IV, *in fine,* in 2010), and Sinaloa (Art. 232, in 2013) among many others, established the same family violence hypothesis.
    The state of Veracruz accounts with the Family Violence Prevention and Assistance Law (*Ley de Asistencia y Prevención de la Violencia Familiar*) and the Boys and Girls Protection and Social Assistance Law (*Ley de Asistencia Social y Protección de Niños y Niñas*), both dated from September 1998, with norms of public and social interest that have the aim of establishing the basis and procedures of assistance and prevention in the topic. A similar legislation was just dictated by the Federation (May 2000). Now, in 2014, all the states of the Republic have legislated on this specific point of children protection.
    Besides, it has been issued the Women General Access Law to a Free Violence Life published in *Diario Oficial de la Federación* on February 1st 2007. This law defines the family violence as 'the abusive act of power or intentional omission in order to dominate, to submit, to control or to injure physically, orally, psychologically, in her patrimony, economically and sexually to women inside or outside the family domicile whose aggressor has or has had a kinship by blood relationship or affinity, marriage, concubinage o having or having had a relationship de facto' (Art. 7). The new law comprehends modalities of violence in the labour, teaching, community and even institutional aspects.
    This law also prevents for the first time, even though in a generic form, a special line to the named *protection directives* or *restriction orders* (cf. *supra,* n. 43). It means the caution acts of urgent application to the subject and which consist in the prohibition of approaching to the domicile, working area, place of studies, or domicile of the victim parents by the probable responsible, the same way the domicile eviction in its case, where they both live together. Nonetheless, the order of protection goes beyond, since it still involves the prohibition to impound or to mortgage goods, in its case.

112. The third obligation of whoever exercises the parental authority lies in the convenient *education of the minor*. Such obligation is found in Article 422 CCDF.

Finally, to protect in an integral manner the minor's personal interests, it is expressly prescribed that the person subject to this authority can neither appear in a trial, nor contract any obligations, without the expressed consent of the titular holders.

113. The following important fact is settled about the effects of the parental authority in relation to the possible goods belonging to the son. These goods that are the property of the son can be of two sorts: Goods that he may acquire because of his job, and goods that he may acquire by any other means.

The goods that he may acquire because of his job belong entirely to the son, even as for its administration and usufruct.

However, the goods of the second class, although they continue to belong entirely to the son, must be administered by the persons who may exercise the parental authority. Besides, the usufruct that eventually exists must be divided into two parts: the first corresponds to the son and the second to the administrators, except in the event that, having acquired these goods by inheritance, legacy, or donation, the testator or donor may have decided in other way.

As it is obvious, the titular holders of the parental authority have the obligation of giving accurate account of the administration of goods referring to.

114. A very important observation which is interesting to mention here, refers to the necessary judicial permission in case of alienation or burden of the goods of the minor. In this case, the law foresees expressly the impossibility to do so without the former authorization, solely because of absolute necessity or evident benefit.

This prohibition is extended to leasing contracts for more than five years, to selling of commercial values and other titles, fruits, and earnings, donation of goods or remission and granting of deposits.

Once the sale has been authorized, the judge has the obligation to observe the destination of the value, establishing expressly that the price of the sale is deposited in an institution of credit. The money cannot be disposed of without a judicial order.

Anyway, the judges always have on their side the faculty to take all measures that are necessary refraining of a disastrous administration of the goods of the son.

Finally, as soon as the minor becomes of age or emancipates, all of his/her goods must be returned to him/her.

115. Logically, parental authority *ends* with the majority of age, that – as it was already mentioned – our Code establishes to be 18 years old. However, it can also end by the emancipation derived from marriage. Let us suppose now that parents may die. If there are no ascendants in the second degree up to that date, then it is presumed that the parental authority must end by impossibility, because there is no

---

Nowadays, all the states which compound the Mexican Republic count on a legislation on this family violence area (Campeche, Chihuahua, San Luis Potosi, Sinaloa and Tamaulipas were the first ones).

other person to whom it must fall. Finally, the parental authority ends with adoption, according to the new Article 443, fr. IV and V, CCDF, in conformity with 2004 reforms.

116. In other cases, it is possible that parental authority simply may be suspended. This can occur when, for instance, the titular is declared interdict, legally absent, judicially condemned to the suspension of the same, or by abuse of alcohol or drugs.[73]

117. A third supposition refers to the *loss* of parental authority. In terms of that set out in Article 444 CCDF, this could occur in the cases of a ruling condemning expressly to the loss of that right; in the cases of divorce; in case of family violence against the minor; disregarding of child support obligation more than ninety days – without any justified cause –; abandoning by the father or the mother of their offspring for more than three months; when whoever exercises it may have committed against the person's or offspring's assets, a crime on purpose or is condemned twice or more times for serious crimes;[74] for unjustified breach of judicial determinations ordered to exercising parental authority designed to correct family violence, when these acts have affected their descendants; and when the child has been wrongfully removed or retained by the person exercising it.

118. A fourth hypothesis lies in the fact of some sort of *limitation* of parental authority. This irregularity in the exercise of right may be a consequence of divorce or separation.

119. Finally, the person designated to exercise the parental authority can validly *excuse* the duty. This happens only in two cases: when the person is 60 years old and when due to illness the charge cannot be duly taken care of.

73. According to the reforms in 2004 and 2008, the parental guardianship can also be suspended when risking health, emotional situation, or life of children; as well as by not living together with the people, whether this agreed by the parties or judicially ordered by any authority; and because of leave the child abandoned (Art. 447, fr. V and VI [2004, 2012] and VII [2008], CCDF).

74. This Art. 444 was again and again reformed. This new 2012 last text is the one which is consigned in the text. A reform in 2007 to the CC of the State of Mexico added the Art. 4.224 to include the hypothesis of recuperation of the parental guardianship when it has been lost by the abandonment of alimony initial duties.

Chapter 7. Guardianship

120. According to Article 449 CCDF 'The purpose of the guardianship is the keeping of the person and goods of those who are not subjected to parental authority and have physical and legal incapacity, or just the second one to govern themselves … '.

Guardianship can also have the objective of the provisional representation of the incapable person (*pupilo*) in very specific cases. These cases, for instance, refer to the necessity to obtain judicial authorization for the alienation, burden or mortgage of minor's real estate and his or her representation in judicial business (Article 643). Another guardian (temporary), the law says, is also required when the guardian and the charge get married without having obtained the necessary exemption. The actuation of this temporary guardian is reduced to the time until the exemption is obtained (Articles 159–160).

However, a temporary guardian is also named while an impediment or excuse is qualified (Article 515). Article 457 refers to a special guardian to defend the interests of the incapable charge when they are opposite to that of other incapable charges under the same guardian, for as long as it takes to decide the point submitted to conflict. It is also possible that a guardian is named exclusively to administer certain goods, for instance, in a testament that institutes as heir a non-protected incapable charge (Article 473). However, if the temporary absence of the testamentary or statutory guardian occurs (Articles 480 and 485), the judge can also provide a temporary guardian.

Another case of naming a temporary guardian is when the guardian ordinarily named cannot give the respective warranty and his/her function is merely reduced to the administration of goods, once received by solemn inventory.

Finally, let us take a look at the case of an incapable charge presenting a judicial complaint against his/her spouse. The law foresees in this case that the judge must appoint a temporary guardian (Article 581 fr. II).[75]

121. So that, the requirement for the forthcoming of the juridical relation generated by this institution is the condition of physical or legal incapacity. Thus, Article 450 reformed states that have natural and legal incapacity the minors, and those adults in state of incapacity, either physical, sensorial, intellectual, emotional, mental or even several of them at once, and cannot manifest their will by themselves or by any other means.

Prior to the reformation of this precept, some denominations that refer to certain kinds of incapacity would use terms that currently would be criticized because of the discrimination involved, such as idiocy, imbecility, etc. (see paragraph 57). Some others expressions were eliminated because of their references to the deaf

75. As for the juridical nature of the guardianship, it is interesting to note that the CCHGO conceptualizes it as a 'juridical act' (Art. 269), while other legislations such as that of Jalisco (Art. 603) and the FCZAC (Art. 408) qualify it as 'an institution of public and social interest and proper to family law.'

mutes, illiterates and habitual drinkers. In virtue of the actual writing, such situation in Mexico City has remained superated.[76]

122. At this point the Code establishes a number of rules that can be systematized in the following form: to begin with, all capable persons have the obligation to perform the responsibility of guardians. Even more, a single guardian can take up to a total of three wards under his/her care, and even more than three, for example under special circumstances, that is, that they may be brothers or heirs of one single person.

What it is forbidden for one single person is to develop simultaneously the charges of guardian and caretaker, and this for the same nature of both charges that, even if complementary between themselves, prosecute different purposes (Article 458; compare Article 618 *in fine*). However, the general rule establishes that the guardianship is done by one tutor, except when there were special circumstances (Article 455, reforms in 2002), because of that, the law already authorizes the plurality in the commission, a situation which was not allowed before. Moral persons can also make the guardianship (Articles 456*bis* and 475).

The kinship implies impossibility as well. To the effect, the Code forbids that people related by virtue of this institution retain among themselves some kind of kinship of a straight line – in any degree – or of collateral line – only up to the fourth degree.

Finally, it is important to mention that the charge of guardian as well as caretaker can neither be confided to functionaries of the familiar court nor to the local counselling of guardianship, or to their relatives.

Therefore, in a generic form, Article 503 CCDF establishes that cannot be guardians: The minors; those of age who are under guardianship; those who may have been removed from another guardianship because of bad behaviour; those who, because of an executed sentence, may have been condemned to the depriving of this charge or the inability to obtain it; those condemned in an executed sentence due to a crime on purpose; those who may not have an honest way of living; those who by transferring the guardianship, may have a pending lawsuit with the own handicapped; the debtors of the handicapped, in a considerable amount; the judges, magistrates and other functionaries or employees of the administration of justice or from the Local Council of Guardianships; those who are not living in the same city; the public servers who due to their functions may have a pecuniary current responsibility; those who may have a disease; and those in general, who the law forbids to do so.

Specifically speaking in relation to the mentally handicapped, cannot be guardians or caretakers of these people who may have provoked such health condition (Article 505).

In 1996, an interesting case was discussed in the following manner: a foreigner, parent of a Mexican minor, claimed before the national justice to not have been

76. On the other hand, the second part of the Art. 462, reformed in 2002, demands the judge to precise, based on the diagnosis of two specialists, the personal legal acts which can effectively make the elder handicapped.

heard in trial in terms of the Vienna Convention on Consular Relations to the consul of his country of origin. The Mexican tribunals solved this in the following way:

> Among the functions of the consuls it is the watching inside the limits that laws may impose and the receiving of State's regulations, for the interests, among other people, of the minors or handicapped who may be nationals from the State that sends the respective consul, particularly when it is required to institute for them a guardianship or a curator; however, such disposition is only applicable when the minors or handicapped may be national, from the State that sends the consul, and not when it is only one of his parents; for if the minors whose guard and custody were the object of natural trial are of Mexican nationality, although one of his parents may be a foreigner, it is evident that the conventional norm appointed previously is not applicable, for there was no obligation on the part of the judge to give intervention in the trial of origin to the consul of the country of origin of the foreign parent.[77]

123. The Code prescribes the taxative division of the guardianship institution in three ways: testamentary, legitimate (or statutory), and *dativa* (or a court-appointed).[78]

124. The first one, that is, the *testamentary* guardianship, is registered in Articles 470–481 CCDF. Thus, the author of a testament has the right to name a guardian in the respective document. If this is so, it is necessary to state that this is the express will of the author, derogating then the legislative limitation that otherwise would run the exercise of the parental authority to the ascendants in second degree (see Article 414 CCDF).

Let us now take a look at the case of naming of a testamentary guardian for a handicapped person. Here there are strict rules that state that if the heir or handicapped person is not under parental authority, an exclusive guardian for the administration of goods can be named. In the same way, the parent who exercises the

---

77. Yves-Marie Luc Gourio Dubos and others [1996] V S.J.F. 477.

78. Only the CC of the states of Morelos (Arts 259 and 284 et seq. [cf. Arts 259 and 284 et seq. CFMOR]) and Nuevo Leon (Arts 461 and 502*bis* et seq.) establish a fourth class denominated *preventative guardianship* and *administration guardianship*, respectively. The first consists in the fact that every person will be able to designate his own guardian in case he may fall in a state of interdiction or into an inability. The second refers, as its name indicates, to the administration of specific goods.

The reforms in Mexico City in 2007 and 2008 prevent now five forms of guardianship, that is to say, the testamentary, statutory, and dativa guardianships, and the *prudential* (Art. 495), and *for children in situation of neglect* guardianships (Art. 461). Therefore, Chapters I*bis* and V are added to the Ninth Title ('On Guardianship'). The fourth one, *prudential* guardianship, is the one referring to the anticipated designation of a guardian, in case of a subsequent incapacity. The fifth and last one, the *children in situation of neglect* guardianship, refers to the children abandoned at birth (Art. 492 CCDF) and it applies through the System for the Family's Integral Development (Sistema para el Desarrollo Integral de la Familia, DIF).

In 1999 Coahuila has made the same and added the *prudential* guardianship and the *auto-designed* guardianship (Arts 558 and 616). Both of them required execution before a notary public (cf. Art. 285 FCMOR).

guardianship of an interdict child, can also name a testamentary guardian, if the mother has passed away or cannot exercise the guardianship legally.

Apart from the cases mentioned in the former paragraph, there is no other case in which the guardianship can take place, via testamentary, of the handicapped person.

125. The second form of guardianship derives from the law and, therefore, it receives the name of *legitimate (or statutory)* guardianship. This form of guardianship is regulated in Articles 482–494 CCDF and takes place only in the cases when there is nobody to exercise the parental authority nor testamentary guardian, and when a guardian must be named because of a divorce situation.

That legitimate guardianship corresponds, in the precise enumeration of the law, only to brethren or other relatives up to the fourth degree.

However, there are some specific cases where the legislator intervenes. For example, between spouses and among grown-up sons in respect of single parents. Parents are also, inversely, in relation to their single sons, but only in cases where there are no grandchildren.

Let us look now, finally, at the case of forced guardianship of the foundling. The law defines the term *foundling* (*expósito*) and distinguishes scrupulously this word from *abandoned* (*abandonado*), this last one which results from the minor whose origin is known. Thus:

> It is considered foundling the minor who is set in a situation of desertion by who, according to law is obliged to his custody, protection and care and his origin cannot be determined. When the situation of desertion refers to a minor whose origin is known, he will be considered abandoned (Article 492, paragraph 2nd, CCDF).

Then, the person who may have sheltered them is designated by law as directly obliged and, being about assistance houses, their directives assume the responsibility, even without previous knowledge of the duties.

126. The *dativa (or a court-appointed)* guardianship, finally, is regulated in Articles 495–499. The *dativa* guardianship takes up this name from the Latin word *datum*, that means give or confer. The *dativa* guardianship takes place in the cases when there is no testamentary guardian or person to whom, according to law, corresponds the statutory guardianship, and when the testamentary guardian is temporarily hindered from exercising his charge. (Article 495).[79]

As a general rule, the naming of this type of guardian is made by the judge of family affairs, but if the minor to protect is 16 years old, it is important to leave the designation made by this last one. When it is about judicial matters of the emancipated minor, the form of guardianship will always be *dativa*. Besides, if it is about minors who are not subjected to parental authority, who may not have a testamentary or legitimate guardian and even if they do not have goods, a dative guardian must be named for them.

79. The Arts 500, 501 and 502 were eliminated in January 2008. They referred to the hypothesis that now is included in the scope of the guardianship for children in situation of neglect.

127. Who must be *separated* from the duty of guardian? According to Article 504 CCDF, will be separated from guardianship those who without having cautioned their management, may exercise the administration of the guardianship; those who are guilty of wrong performance of guardianship, either regarding the person, or with respect to the administration of the goods of the wards; the guardians who may neither exhibit the medical certificates nor surrender their information and accounts in term; those incapables for exercising the guardianship; the guardian who wants to married the ward; the guardian absent from the city for more than three months; and the guardian who may exercise family violence or may commit a crime on purpose against the ward.

The act of separation can be promoted by the Public Prosecutor, in its character of social representative, or else by the wards relatives.

128. There are some people who may *excuse* themselves for the performance of the function according to Article 511. They are the public officials; the militaries in active service; those who have under their parental authority three or more descendants; those who due to their socio-economical situation, may not attend to the guardianship without affecting their subsistence; those under habitual bad conditions of health; those who are 60 years old; those who have another guardianship or curatorship; and those persons lacking experience, and not capable to carry out the guardianship.

The excuse must be evaluated precisely in the term that is fixed by the Civil Procedures Code, that is, immediately or within the following twenty-four hours from gaining knowledge of the facts regarding the impediment (Article 171 CPCDF).

129. Due to the specific nature of the charge, the law demands the granting of *warranties*. These may consist in a mortgage, pledge or deposit, according to Articles 519 and 526, that subdue the precedence of the deposit only when there are no goods to constitute the mortgage or the pledge. However, it is also true that a mixed system can be adopted, this is, that it is given partially in mortgage and pledge, and partially in deposit.

These warranties will cover an amount enough to cover the responsibility for the managing, according to the value of the rents, goods and products.

Anyway, it is clearly understood that if the goods of the handicapped person suffer increment or decrement, the warranty will have the same fate (Article 529).

However, there will be certain people who are not obliged to give a warranty, according to the foresaid in Article 520. They are the testamentary guardians, when the testator has expressly relieved them of this obligation; the tutor who does not manage any goods; the father, the mother and grandparents, when they are called to perform the guardianship of their descendants; and those who may shelter a foundling, feed him and educate him conveniently for more than ten years.

To these cases must be added those of the spouses, ascendants or sons, and also the case of the joint heir except where the authorities decide otherwise or when his or her share is not enough in this last case.

So, in this way, it is interesting to note specially that the judge responds with the guardian to the consequential damages and loss of profits that the handicapped person may undergo for not having demanded the caution.[80]

130. What are the main obligations of the guardian? Article 537 appoints that the guardian is obliged to feed and educate the ward; to address preferably the resources of the physically challenged for illicit substances, to the healing of his diseases and to his rehabilitation; to form solemn inventory of the minor's or handicapped's goods in not more than six months; to administer the property; to represent the handicapped in a trial and out of it in all the civil acts (with exception to marriage, child's recognition, testament and other strictly personal affairs); and to request ahead of time the necessary judicial authorization for all business that he cannot do legally without.

Precisely, one of the first provisions that the guardian must adopt once he recognizes charge, consists of the obligation to give food and education to the ward.

In this respect, the judge must fix the necessary amount and this must be followed, logically, in relation to the principle of satisfaction of such needs according to his or her personal condition and economical possibilities. A very important disposition is stated in Article 545 which transfers to the government the obligation of to provide food and education of the indigent handicapped person, unless relatives are located, in which case expenses must be recovered.

The obligation to make inventory is regulated in Article 537, fr. III, already commented, and in Articles 548–553. Of course, one of the most important functions of the guardian is the protection of this patrimony. Therefore, the Code imposes the legally binding condition to conserve such goods unless there is a cause of absolute necessity or an evident utility of the ward and even submits the sale of real estate to public pawn. Such dispositions must relate to Articles 436 and 437, for the distinct case of parental authority.

131. A judicial license is required for the case of extraordinary expenses, transactions, compromise in arbiters, payment of credits, cession of rights (but in these last two cases only in favour of the guardian), leasing for more than five years, and reception of loans and donations.[81] However, inversely, the guardian has the obligation to accept simple donations, succession rights and legacies in favour of the charge (Article 579).

132. Logically, the guardian has the right to receive a payment and the Code is clear in the sense that such payment must not be less than five or exceed 10% of the taxable rents that the goods may suppose. However, the only limitation lies in the prohibition to contract marriage, because in that case he/she must restitute what he/she may have received.

80. According to a reform in 2007 in Mexico City, when they were two persons the responsible of the guardianship, both have to respond together in favour of the handicapped (Art. 530).
81. A reform in 2007 in Mexico City authorizes the charged of the guardianship to pay the urgent medical services without demanding any other authorization (Art. 565).

It is also true that this retribution may increment up to 20% if guardian skills for the patrimonial increment is proven for two consecutive years. The reform in 2007 permits retribution to be divided when two persons exercise the charge (Article 585*bis*).

133. It has already been mentioned that one of the main obligations of the guardian is to appropriately inform the judge. The Code details this obligation in Articles 590–605 insisting on the serious responsibility of the same and settling specific obligations for guilt or negligence in the development of such obligation. This obligation cannot be dispensed and it even passes on to the heirs.

134. The guardianship is ended at the ward's death or when the incapacity ceases; but it can also end by the situation coming under parental authority, either for recognition, or for adoption (Article 606).

Once the guardianship has ended, the guardian has two important tasks: first, the return of the goods, and second, the provision of information according to law.

The guardian continues to maintain his responsibility for a total of four years. This term is counted from the day when the minor becomes of age, or when the goods and accounts may have been received, or from the ceasing of the incapacity.

135. The Code devotes yet a special chapter (Chapter XIV, Articles 618–630 'On the curador') to the regulation of the figure of the caretaker or conservator (*curador*).[82] The word *curatela* comes from the Latin word *curare*, that means take care or protect. Therefore, by means of this function an observer is instituted in order to survey the guardian, with regard at all times the permanent protection of the charge.

The CCDF foresees the obligations of the caretaker. Thus, in the terms of Article 626, the caretaker is obliged to defend the rights of the handicapped, in a trial or out of it, exclusively in the case that they are in opposition to those of the guardian; to observe the conduct of the guardian and to inform the judge; to inform the judge too of the naming of the guardian, when he was absent or he may abandon the guardianship; and to accomplish all other related obligations. The caretaker who may not accomplish the duties foreseen in this Article will be responsible of compensatory damages and loss of profits that may result to the handicapped person.[83]

Who may be designated caretaker? To begin with, it is the general rule foreseen in Article 623, which establishes that whoever has the right to name a guardian, can also name a caretaker. The caretaker of other individuals must be named by the

---

82. The *curatela* is an institution of common acceptance in our legislation; there are only three cases where it is not foreseen, that is, in the CC of Quintana Roo, Tamaulipas, and in the FC of Hidalgo. The reforms made in Mexico City (2002), Morelos (2006), Michoacan (2008), and Sinaloa (2013) preserve this figure.

83. Some other codes consign specific obligations for the caretaker. Among these obligations are: demanding judicially that the managing of the parental authority be guaranteed (Art. 641 fr. II, CCTAB; Art. 473, fr. II CCTLAX; and Art. 589, fr. II, FCZAC); satisfy the particular obligations that the testator may have imposed to him eventually (Art. 510, fr. IV, CCYUC); and specially to watch the state of the landed property goods mortgaged or delivered in pledge by the author (Arts 656 CCBCS and 355, fr. IV *in fine*, FCMOR).

judge, and even this functionary has the faculty to approve of the designation of those older than 16 years may do so concerning his/her *dativa* guardianship and the minors emancipated because of marriage.[84]

136. In Mexico City a Local Guardianship Council (Consejo Local de Tutelas) functions as a surveillance and information organ. It has the following obligations: to form and remit to the judges of family matters a list of the people who may perform the guardianship; to look after the guardians' duties accomplishment, specially education and assistance, giving notice to the judge; to let the judge know when the handicapped's goods are in danger; to investigate who are the handicapped who lack a guardian; to take care specially that guardians accomplish his/her obligation about minor's health; and to watch the registry of guardianships (Article 632 CCDF).

In practice, however, the integration and the functioning of these local guardianships councils are very limited. In the states the matter is still more difficult, even in the large cities and, of course, its functioning is ineffective in rural communities and remote villages.

84. In the amendment in 2002 in Mexico City, it was established that the curatorship can also be conferred to moral persons. Moreover, it was established that the foundling or abandoned children will not obtain the curatorship (Art. 618).

Chapter 8. Kinship and Relationships of Affinity

137. Regarding kinship, it is important to mention that our Code extensively enumerates the lines and degrees in which such situation is produced. Thus, an entire chapter of the Civil Code (Chapter I, Title VI, 'On kinship', Articles 292–300) is devoted to this topic.[85]

Three types of kinship are recognized in our country: related by consanguinity, related by affinity, and related by civil law.

138. The *related by consanguinity kinship* is the one that is commonly called by the people kinship 'of blood'. It is established among the people who descend from the same parent and maintains two directions, one ascendant and another descendant. Ascendants are parents, grandparents, great-grandparents, etc., and descendants are children, grandchildren, great-grandchildren, and so forth.[86]

The way counting in this case is quite simple, because every generation forms a degree. However, the people who may exist from one extreme to the other, excluding the parent in this case can also be counted.

However, the straight or transversal line is compounded by all of the degrees that may exist among people who, without descending from the others, proceed nevertheless from a single common trunk. It may be either equal or unequal. It refers to brethren, uncles, aunts, nephews, nieces, cousins, and so forth. In this case, it is easy as well to count: one moves up on one line and descends on the other, according to the extremes sought. It can also apply only to persons, but in this case it must be taken out to the progenitor.

It must be clarified at this point that due to the relative reformations to adoption, the adoption will be compared in all forms to the blood-related kinship. Thus, the Code says that it is 'as if the adopted were a blood related child'. In this same case, it is also compared the parental relationship by blood, to the relation produced between the child adopted, the person adopting, the family of this and the descending people of that one (Articles 293 *in fine,* 390, 395, I, II, and 396 CCDF).[87]

139. However, the following form of kinship is established precisely in view of marriage, excluding, of course, the spouses themselves. This is the named *affinity kinship.* In this way, the male establishes kinship with the relatives of the woman, and the woman, at the same time, establishes kinship with the male's relatives.

85. The FCHGO is the only one which defines general kinship in the following terms: 'Kinship is the subsisting link between the members of a family' (Art. 151). The rest of the other civil and family codes it defines in a particular form (as consanguinity, affinity, and civil kinship).

86. The reform in 2007 compares the parental blood relationship to the other one produced between the child born by assisted reproduction and the ones who have to be reputed as the progenitors. However, the full donation of germinal cells does not generate any parental relationship between the donator and the product (Arts 293, para. 2nd, CCDF, and 198 FCSIN).

87. The new FCSIN just recognize two types of kinship, that is to say, by consanguinity and by affinity. The third one, civil kinship – that becomes only for adoption –, it was indeed subsumed under the first one (Arts 196 and 199 CFSIN, 2013). Nevertheless, this tendency is not followed by the 2010 Aguascalientes reforms (Art. 413 CCAGS).

Thus, it is mentioned brothers-in-law, parents-in-law, daughters-in-law and sons-in-law to specify what is generally called in Mexico 'political' relatives (the in-laws).[88]

140. Finally, the *civil kinship* is that one established only from adoption, according to the great majority of provincial civil codes, and indeed, in the City of Mexico. That is the sense or Article 295 CCDF, but delimited in the term of Article 410-D, now repealed, but in force in the Articles 395, II and 293 already mentioned.

In other parts of the Code some juridical consequences relative to kinship are mentioned as well. Thus, such isolated precepts must relate to this homogeneous block from this Title VI to obtain the systematic analysis of the whole institution. In this way, it is about the kinship in the impediments for the celebration of marriage and for the exercise of the functions proper from the guardian and caretaker, as well as the relative to the successory subject.

88. Now, the CCTLAX (Art. 139) states that 'It is also existing the kinship by affinity in the relation that results in view of the concubinage, among the concubinary and the relatives of the concubine and among the relatives of both, hers and his. This assimilation only includes consanguineous relatives in a straight line, ascendant or descendant, without any limitation in degree; and its only effect is to constitute an impediment for marriage.' This normative is followed by the FCZAC (Art. 248) and the CC of Guerrero (Art. 379), Tabasco (Art. 290), Federal District (Art. 294) and, in a generical form, by the FCSIN (Arts 168 and 173).

Part III. Matrimonial Property Law

Chapter 1. Rights and Obligations of Spouses

§1. General Principles

141. We have already mentioned that the rights and obligations of spouses are condensed in several principles of general application. Among them we can find the following foreseen in law:

142. The principle of mutual help. It is found stipulated in Article 147, although in a negative sense, because it is stated that any condition that results contrary to this duty will be perceived as not settled. It is clear that this duty of mutual help means the reciprocal collaboration to face the everyday problems that result from a union that is formed by two people at the beginning, then after years will increase eventually not only with children, but also reaching sometimes, as regularly happens in Mexico, multiple derivations that include grandchildren, grandparents and other relatives of a 'political' character.

This principle is also reinforced by Article 162, where in a positive sense now, it is established that spouses are obliged to contribute to the aims of marriage and to mutual help.

143. The principle of perpetuation of the species. Thus, the following principle that directly results from the formation of this union precisely to the descendant, that is, to birth, formation and development of new beings who are the product of that union.

144. The principle of living together. However, Article 163 establishes in a brief and definite form that 'The spouses will live together in the marital domicile'. Following, the concept of marital domicile is defined, stating that it is 'the place established in a common agreement by spouses, in which both enjoy their own authority and equal considerations' (compare Article 67, paragraph 2nd, FCSIN, 2013).

145. The principle of economical contribution. At the same time, Article 164 establishes the economical obligation that both spouses have under their charge in the different aspects that comprehend the formation of a home. This refers, mainly, to the sustenance of the same, to the alimony of the spouses and that of their children, as well as the education of the latter.

This economical contribution does not have to be necessarily equal. In fact, in a society still so traditional as the Mexican one – specially in the rural areas – it is not rare to find that the male carries the economical load of home, as the woman contributes to the children's care and the attention of the domestic necessities, as well as the person and goods of the husband.

But besides this real fact, the law establishes as well as an exception the fact that one of them is unable to work and besides lacks goods of his or her property. In this case the other must contribute in a total way with the domestic work and expenses. Such exception, however, does no more than confirm the noble principle of mutual help in a freely chosen union.

146. Finally, *the principle of equality*. However, it is true that independent of the economical contribution, the spouses possess a formal equality about their authority and relations with one another. Thus, Article 168 says that 'The husband and the wife will have authority at home and equal considerations.' The same precept clarifies that the space where this authority must be exercised equally is expressed in the managing of the home, in the formation and education of children, and in the administration of goods.

§2. The Household Expenses

147. We have already mentioned that the Code expressly prevents in its Article 164 and 164*bis* the form providing for household expenses. The law says, indeed, that the spouses will contribute economically to the home support, to their alimony and to the children support, as well as their education, distributing the load in form and rate according to their possibilities. As we said, this will not apply to the person who has not the capacity to work and having no goods. These rights and obligations will always be equal for the couple and independent of their economical contribution to the home support. (Article 164.)

Certainly, the new tendency in this issue is to consider the domestic work and the guard of children as economical contribution to the home support. (Article 164*bis*)

The FC of Hidalgo (Article 46) and Sinaloa (Articles 69 and 127), the CCMEX (Articles 4.18, paragraph 3rd; 4.46, paragraph 2nd and 4.99), CCAGS (Article 310*bis*), CCQRO (Article 268), CCCOAH (Article 367) and the CCDF (Articles 164*bis* and 267) already recognize this servant job of the female partner, and it compares to the male job.

§3. The Matrimonial Home

148. However, Article 163 CCDF establishes the provision about the matrimonial home. It is interesting now to place this concept in the widest frame of the dispositions concerning the home contained in the Code. Thus, this precise concept of matrimonial home must be framed up in the context foreseen by Articles 29–34 that refers to the home in general, to the assumption of residence, to the diverse causes of reputation of the legal home, as well as to the conventional character, besides the derogated cause of divorce that consisted of the separation of the matrimonial home for more than six months without any justified cause, or for more than a year even with a cause (Article 267, fr. VIII and IX CCDF, now repealed, but in force yet in the majority of provincial codes).

However, Article 267, fr. IV form part of this context that establishes the necessity to appoint the home that will serve as residence for each of the spouses during the process of divorce, and Article 310 that in matter of food foresees the incorporation into the family of the alimentary creditor, not forgetting that in this last hypothesis it cannot be described as the matrimonial home any more.

A rather peculiar institution is the *family patrimony*, which has as an objective the affectation of one or more goods to the economical protection of the family. In general, this economical protection is focused to the home of spouses and children including, of course, the household items.[89] To be effective, the patrimony in Mexico City will not overtake the amount of MXN 2,210,476 (USD 165,000 approximately, to February 2014).[90] Any family member can become part of this patrimony in affectation, but once it has been formed, the goods become inalienable, imprescriptible and impoundable. It is obligatory that for its formation a family judge and a notary public intervene – in this last case, when any real estate goods in the patrimony were involved.

The formation of the family patrimony cannot be made in fraud to others, of course, and it has to be finished when, for instance, the beneficiaries will not become food creditors or stop living, cultivating, or using the house, the lot, or the business premises any more, for one year.

§4. Transactions between Spouses

149. There is a very specific regulation in the Civil Code about transactions between spouses. The general principle is found established in Article 172 which states that both spouses have the entire capacity to make business and to exercise all type of legal actions, without requiring each other's consent for it, except in relation to the acts of administration and of dominium of the common goods.

This last addition, however, causes some problems. Thus, the husband and wife can celebrate among themselves a sale, but only when the patrimonial regime is under separation of goods. Nevertheless, a new law in Zacatecas already allows this contract, even under the community property regime (Articles 131, fr. I, a, and 133 CFZAC, 2009).

Since January 1997, an important reform in the state of Veracruz demands that both spouses acquire in a 'simultaneous way' before a notary public the dominion of goods and the title of rights, which acquire only then the character of common, and therefore, cannot be the object of division as long as the relationship subsists.

89. In some cases it also includes in rural environments the cultivable plot and some industrial, commercial, and agricultural, family business. In fact, a reform in 1996 to the CCJAL permits to include an auto-motor vehicle (Art. 777), and in other cases, the home, furniture, animals, personal property, as well as professional jobs and occupations handwork (Arts 723 CCDF and 581 FCSIN).

90. In the new FCSIN the amount is MXN 2,614,570 (USD 195,000 approximately). (Art. 584 FCSIN).

Thus, these goods or rights cannot be alienated without the intervention of both spouses.

Let us now look at what happens with gifts. To start off, it is established that the spouses can make donations to each other, but only as long as they are not contrary to the matrimonial capitulations. Now then, an important limitation is established, that is, that these gifts can be revoked if there is a justified cause, under judgment of the judicial authority. As it is clear, such gifts can only be revoked during the validity of marriage and, once the matrimonial link is dissolved, it must be understood that they remain firm in a definite form.

Finally, Article 234 foresees that these donations between spouses cannot even be ineffective in case of new children coming to them. However, they can be reduced in case of *inoficiosidad.* That is, when it is not observed the children support obligation (see again Articles 221, 234, 1374 and 2348 CCDF).

Chapter 2. The Marriage Settlement

150. In Mexico the institution of the necessary prenuptial agreement on gifts (or *dote*) does not exist anymore, although in any case it is important to clarify that in the indigenous customs of the rural communities there still subsist a series of pacts about the fact, but little by little, they will transfer the road to the common norms of the Civil Code.

What the Code does permit is donations precisely given in consideration of the future marriage. Thus, they are called *pre-marriage* donations. The Code defines them in its Article 219 stating that pre-marriage donations are those done before marriage between the future spouses, and those that a third party does to any or both of the future spouses, precisely in consideration to marriage.

All those presents made precisely in consideration to the wedding maintain that same limitation, that is, they will not have any value if the marriage is not carried out. In this case, the law says that such donations will remain *without effect.*

There is as well another important limitation. It refers to the amount donated. In this case the Civil Code says that all reunited donations must not exceed a sixth part of the goods of whoever makes the donation.[91] The pre-marital donations are not revoked, diversely, because children may come to the donor, because it is already understood that they are precisely confirmed with the celebration of marriage.

We would like to clarify precisely the extent of this last assertion. Article 230 states that the pre-marital donations remain without effect if the marriage is not carried out, but it is convenient to state that even after celebrating the wedding, and therefore acquiring efficiency in the respective donation, it may however be revoked – and in fact, the law assumes that it is so – because of the adultery, family violence, unjustified abandoning of the alimony obligation, and other ones evenly serious.[92]

At the end, as is seen, the contradiction is justly apparent. Both dispositions conform a harmonious regime, thus protecting the final consideration of the act and the protection to the juridical sphere of the hypothetical victim.

Contrary to general donations (Article 2340), the donations of a pre-marital character do not require expressed acceptance; it is enough just with a tacit acceptance that must of course be credited with the possession of the thing or rights and the absence of its abandoning or resignation (Article 225).

It should be emphasized, in relation to this matter, that our law grants the term of a year for the couple who never got married to have among themselves the right to demand the devolution of that donated. The term of a year must be counted from the separation of the fiancées and not from the date when the wedding was supposed to be celebrated. Nevertheless, this chapter about fiancées (Articles 139–145) has already been derogated, but only in the CCDF and a few provincial codes.

Finally, it is necessary to say at this point regarding the marriage settlement, that in our family law the prenuptial agreement which sets forth the patrimonial rights of each person in case of a future divorce does not exist.

91. Most of laws in the Mexican Republic state that the donations in the betrothal cannot exceed of a sixth part of the donor. In Jalisco they are reduced to a fifth part (Art. 360 CCJAL).
92. The FCZAC (Art. 180, October 2007) and FCSIN (Art. 77, August 2013) have established the same thing.

Chapter 3. Conventional Matrimonial Regimes

151. Our Civil Code states expressly that the contract of matrimony must be celebrated under the regime of *community property* or under *separation of goods.*[93]

In virtue of the first, the regime of community property makes the goods that they are owners of, enter a patrimonial fund, not only at that moment, but also those that they may acquire in the future.

On the other hand, in virtue of the second, the regime of separation of goods, the spouses maintain the property and the administration of the goods that in virtue of the capitulations belong to them, as well as the interest that the same produce.[94]

The origin of the patrimonial regime is found in the capitulations. The word *capitulation* comes from the word *capitular* that means 'pact or agreement'. In virtue of these capitulations the spouses – or even the fiancées if they are celebrated before marriage – agree on the conditions to constitute one or other regime, as the case may be.

As it was said, these matrimonial capitulations may be celebrated even before the wedding, but it may also be done simultaneously with its celebration. Until recently, in practice those fiancées and spouses who actually agree on this situation were very scant.

152. The matrimonial capitulations on which the *community property* is agreed must observe a series of points.

So, the contract must contain a detailed list of the real property goods that every spouse may take to the society, with its value and its taxation report; the list of the movable goods that every spouse contributes to the society; note of personal debts; whether the marital society may have to include all goods of every spouse or only part of them; whether marital society may include all the goods of the spouses or just their products; whether the labour product of every spouse corresponds exclusively to whoever executed it, or if he must give participation of that product to the other spouse and in what proportion; the declaration if both spouses, or only one of

93. The most recent movement of ideas on this point regulates three more economical regimes, besides the community property and the separation of goods. They are named the 'economical mixed regime', the 'legal community', and the 'additional legal regime', but there are not many important differences among them.

Indeed, the generality of the civil codes of our country clearly define the regimes of community property and separation of goods; the other civil and family codes of the Republic that define certain special regimes – that may differ or not – are the FC of the states of Zacatecas (Art. 135), Morelos (Art. 141 [cf. Art. 95 FCMOR]), and Hidalgo (Art. 60), and the CC of Jalisco (Art. 282) and Sonora (Art. 270), all of them under the denomination of *mixed* or *legal* regime.

The CC of Aguascalientes (Art. 175), Oaxaca (Art. 178) and Yucatan (Art. 117) only modify the current denomination to adopt the classification of *legal* or *voluntary* society regime. The CC of San Luis Potosi does not seem to foresee any expressed division about it, but any way it defines the goods that will be proper of every one of the spouses and those others who will be common (Arts 163 et seq.).

94. But there is an important and newly exception, that is, when the house is habited by both spouses, because in this case the conjugal authorization before notary public is required (Art. 72 *in fine*, CFSIN, 2013).

them will administer the society, expressing the faculties that in its case are conceded, in a clear form; the declaration about the future goods that the spouses may acquire during marriage; what to do with the future assets acquired by inheritance, legacy, donation, or gift of fortune; and the basis to finish with the society (Article 189).

If it concerns real property goods, the capitulations must be formalized in a deed before a notary public and besides must be registered in the Public Property's Register, to give effect before a third party.

There are, however, some specific dispositions that complement the provisions of Article 189. Thus, for instance, the necessity to complement the consent of the minor is established.

153. It is necessary to add as well, that the lack of formality in a deed produces of course the relative voiding of the act, which, of course, does not refrain the act from being carried out duly afterwards.[95]

Capitulations may be void as well, when, for example, it is established that only one of the spouses must perceive all of the earnings, or that only one may be responsible for the losses, gains and debts, when they exceed a certain proportionality.

Earnings that eventually result from the society cannot be quitted either and in such sense, the agreed stipulation would be void.

Finally, it is necessary to examine the different situation of ceasing of the effects of the conjugal society. In this case, it is established expressly that the abandoning without any justification of the conjugal domicile for more than six months causes the partial inefficiency of the favourable effects in relation to the spouse who abandons. This disposition must also be related to that set out in Articles 698–704, where it is expressly stated that the declaration of absence constitutes a cause of interruption of the conjugal relationship.

154. What are the effects of voiding? Naturally, nothing can be decided until an executed sentence has been pronounced, so that the relationship is considered as subsistent in its terms. However, if there had been bad faith from any of the spouses, the relationship may only subside if the continuation is favourable to the innocent spouse. Now, if it is not so, and the subsistence of the effects of the relationship eventually throws prejudice on this last one, the executed sentence brings back its effects and is considered void from the very beginning, and this case is analogue to the one that results if both spouses may have proceeded with bad faith, because then only the third party's rights remain secure.

There is another consequence important in itself as well: The spouse who may work in bad faith does not take part in the earnings after the dissolution of the relationship. In this way, the earnings are applied to children, and in some cases, to the innocent spouse. If both proceeded in bad faith, the authorities just apply to the children. Articles 203–206 define rules of specific application for the case of formation of inventories, credit payments and destination of losses.

95. Because of a reform in 2004 in Mexico City, now the capitulations can already be given or modified in judicial venue or notary public venue, in this last case through a public deed, in terms of what it is established in the Art. 180.

Finally, it has been added the Article 206*bis* emphasizing the need of the consent of both to sell, to rent or to transfer the common goods. However, now it is warned that the operation can be completed by just one of them, even though with a legal authorization. It is the case of the spouse abandoned who requires food for themselves or their sons.

155. The *termination* of the community property may come from a series of stipulated causes, not without a certain disorder, in Articles 187–188 and 197. Under this scheme, it is understood immediately that the most important cause of dissolution is, of course, the personal dissolution of the marriage; but it may come from the free will of the spouses, as well, or from the change of regime.

There are, of course, peculiar cases. Thus, Article 188 states that the conjugal society may end also during marriage, by the request of any of the spouses, if one of the spouses, due to his notorious negligence in the administration of goods, threatens to ruin the other; when one of the spouses, without the other's consent, makes cession of goods to creditors; if one of the spouses is declared bankrupt; and for any other reason according to the judge.

Finally, the sentence that declares the presumption of death of the absent spouse (Article 713) provokes the termination as well.

156. Now, on the other hand, the *separation of goods* constitutes, as has already been expressed, the case precisely contrary to the community property. It is important to note that, in practice, more and more a larger number of couples prefer this regime, although it is certain that previously the large majority of marriages chose the joint marriage. It is also clear that an important reason resides in the fact that, not celebrating capitulations, many codes in the Republic establish the legal presumption that the patrimonial regime is constituted under the conjugal contract (see *infra*, paragraph 159).

The separation of goods may adopt a double meaning. In the first case, the separation of goods may be absolute, in which hypothesis nothing is shared by the spouses; in a second case the separation of goods is only partial and in this modality it attends then, from the strictly legal point of view, a mixed regime that comprehends simultaneously a separation of goods in respect to some properties and a society in respect to that not excluded.

157. Logically, the reasons that may establish the separation must be submitted in a public notice if such is the case, except for the celebration of it before marriage. In any case, they will contain a specific inventory of every one of the goods of exclusive property as well as debts.

158. The most important juridical consequence of separation has to do, of course, with the exclusive property of goods. Thus, interest on the goods continues to belong to the proprietary spouse. It is expressly established that every one of the spouses acquires and administrates exclusively the earnings by personal services.

There is one very important exception. It refers to the case when spouses acquire jointly because of donation, inheritance, legacy, gift of fortune or any other free title.[96] The administration, in this case, corresponds to both and now it is understood that it must be proceeded to the adequate division.

None of the spouses may require the other for the payment of honoraries for personal services. This is the general rule, but it has an important exception in Article 216 *in fine*, CCDF (2000), that says that the spouse temporarily in charge of the administration of the property of the absent or disabled person is entitled to being compensated for his or her service – in proportion to its importance and results (compare too Article 128 FCSIN, 2013).

96. The CCMEX and the FCSIN indeed state the same donation, inheritance, legacy, and gift of fortune, but both codes make addition of prescription, credits and rights –both acquired before marriage-, goods exchange, mergers, author's rights and personal property (Art. 182*quintus*, CCDF; Art. 4.27 CCMEX, 2010 and Arts 94 and 126 FCSIN, 2013).

Chapter 4. The Legal Matrimonial Regime

159. We have stated before that law concedes to the spouses the possibility to expressly agree on the marital capitulations that they find convenient, either to construct a community property, or to agree on the separation of goods. In any case, the capitulations define the patrimonial situation of the goods.

The law itself is extensive in the provision of the requirements that must be observed in the celebration of these capitulations. It is said for example that, the agreements that may involve the transfer of landed property goods, as well as their respective inscription in the Public Property's Register, must be stated in a general notice before a notary public. According to that set out in Article 189, the capitulations must follow a long series of requirements that were mentioned in paragraph 152.

Now, the law establishes the disposition that everything which is not expressly stipulated, must be remitted to the general dispositions of the community property (Article 183 CCDF). Article 98 fr. V states that along with the marital request it must be necessary to accompany the agreement that pretenders celebrate in relation to their goods. The nature of the convention must be clearly expressed.

Other legislations, instead, are much more specific in that sense. Thus, for example, the CCVER establishes in its Article 166 the following:

> Marriage must be celebrated under the regime of community property, or under the one of separation of goods. Under lack of capitulations to define one or another, the law establishes the legal presumption that marriage has been celebrated under the regime of community property.[97]

Besides, this same legal body repeats in its Article 17, that once the case of legal presumption is applied, the precepts that by analogy must be applied are those relative to society and the co-property, as to how applicable they might be.

Nonetheless, recent amendments in this provincial code, which we have already commented on (*supra*, paragraph 149), demands the requirement of 'simultaneity' before the notary public by both spouses for its consideration as a good of common nature.

---

97. Community property is certainly the general rule that states the normative of the following codes: CC from the states of Nuevo Leon (Art. 178), Chihuahua (Art. 165), Puebla (Art. 338), Morelos (Art. 141 [cf. Art. 95 CFMOR]), Tabasco (Art. 180) and Quintana Roo (Art. 719). The presumption derives on favour of the modality of the so named 'legal society' in the case of the following legislations: CC from Tamaulipas (Art. 172), Oaxaca (Art. 206), Jalisco (Art. 282), Aguascalientes (Art. 209), Sonora (Art. 270) and FC of Sinaloa (Art. 86).

    Nevertheless, on the other hand, the following codes expressly prevent the presumption in a directly contrary sense: FCHGO (Art. 60), CC of Yucatan (Art. 117), Zacatecas (Art. 138), Guanajuato (Art. 176), Queretaro (Art. 166), Guerrero (Art. 437), Campeche (Art. 189), Michoacan (Art. 173 (cf. Art. 202 CFMICH]) and Tlaxcala (Art. 60) because then the separation of goods will be established, with the legal effects of the case.

    The rest of the codes do not contain express provisions in this sense.

Part IV. Succession Law

Chapter 1. Intestate Succession

§1. The Opening of the Succession

I. Death

160. In terms stated in Article 1599 CCDF, the intestate succession is opened when there is no will, or the one which was granted was void or lost its worth; when the testator did not dispose of all assets; when the imposed condition to the heir is not accomplished; and when the heir dies before the testator; he repudiates the inheritance; or he is incapable of inheriting.

The moment when the inheritance is differed, must go back to the decedent's death. Therefore, there is not in Mexican law about what in other systems are known as *laying inheritance*. Accurately, Article 1649 of the CCDF states that 'The succession is opened at the moment when the decedent dies.' However, the diverse Article 1660 states that 'The effects of acceptance or disclaim of the inheritance are always brought back to the date of the heir's death. Such dispositions are repeated in the Article 1290 for the specific case of legacies.

The hereditary mass is confirmed as a common patrimony in favour of the heirs, keeping in this way its integrity up to the moment at which the division has to be made. Therefore, the heirs may effectively make use of the right they may have in the hereditary mass *in abstracto*, but they cannot make use materially of the things that integrate the common property.

Thus, Article 2047 states that by transferring the right to an inheritance, there is an obligation to answer only the exclusive quality of the heir, if the things that are part of it are not numbered or conveniently identified. Besides, the successors – advises Article 1665 – cannot alienate their rights until after the death of the decedent.

There is, nevertheless, an important limitation. This refers to the preferential right that the coheirs keep in the case of selling hereditary rights. In this way, the assumed seller must notify by means of a notary public, judge, or before two witnesses, the basis on which the sale has been concerted. The coheirs have a term of eight days to make their right worth. The sanction in case of possible omission is rather serious because if the sale takes place, it will be void.

II. Missing Persons and Absentees

161. As for the cases of absentees, there are specific dispositions about the faculties conceded to the presumptive heir, who may be named as absentee's depositary or representative. It is certain, however, that there is a specific order in Articles 653 and 659, where preference is given to the spouse, descendants or ascendants, but if all of them are lacking, the assumed heir may be designated.

In any case, the presumptive heir will have the faculties and the obligations that correspond to the charge, and at the right moment, legal declaration of absence may be requested. In this case, the legitimate heirs keep even a preference right in front of other heirs, for example, by virtue of a will, according to the formulation of Article 653.

Such request must be published during a period of three months, every fifteen days, in the official newspaper that may correspond and in the main newspaper of the city. After four months, counted from the last publication, if there was neither news nor an opposition from any person with legitimate interest, the judge will declare the legal absence. This declaration of absence must be published one more time and it even must be repeated every two years until the assumption of death is declared.

However, it is enough with the declaration of absence, for the legitimate assumed heirs to be then put in provisional possession of the goods that form the hereditary mass, confirming the designation done in favour of any of them from the naming of specific depositary or representative.

In this case, there is the problem of whether or not the goods may be given a comfortable division. If they are susceptible to being easily divided, it is quite clear that every one will possess and administrate the part that corresponds to him/her; on the contrary, if they are not easily divisible, the heirs will have to select among themselves a general administrator.

162. The CCDF establishes in its Article 705 a term of six years as a minimum for the declaration of assumption of death. But this general rule has some exceptions, in case of catastrophies such as war, shipwrecks, floods or any other accident of a similar character, because in these cases two years will be enough and the previous declaration of absence is even considered as unnecessary.

There are even more extreme cases: They refer to the founded assumption that the disappearance or death may have occurred because of a fire, explosion, earthquake or aerial or railroad accident, because in these hypotheses the passing of six months is sufficient.[98]

163. Now, we shall ask what happens in the case of the eventual rights of the absent person? To start off, the Code demands proof regarding the existence of the person precisely at the time when the right must have been acquired. A specific case that the Code deals with is precisely that which refers to the succession in an inheritance. Thus, if the hereditary successor is declared absent or even assumed dead, a

98. Cf. Art. 150 CCPUE, 2010, to the case of organized delinquency. And still, a reform in 2007 in Jalisco it decreases the term only to three months (Art. 146).

rigorous inventory of the goods susceptible as the transmission must be made, now with respect to the coheirs of the assumed absent or dead person. His/her condition in the succession will acquire the characteristics of provisional possession or be definite according to the time in which the inheritance is transmitted in relation to the process of absence or assumption of death.

Anyway, according to Article 718 CCDF, the rights for the action of petition of inheritance remain secure, not only on the part of the absent person or his/her representative, but also on the part of the creditors or heirs as well.

§2. The Heir

I. Capacity to Succeed

164. Obviously, all persons have a capacity to inherit. This is the general rule stated in Article 1313 CCDF, which besides prevents specifically the irrelevance of the age of the assumed heir (remember, also, that Article 22 CCDF states the thesis of the *nasciturus*).

In any case, there are some particular causes by virtue of which certain people may be deprived of their right to inherit. These reasons will be analysed next (*infra*, paragraph 166).

II. Simultaneous Death

165. In this natural phenomenon, simultaneous death, the law establishes in its Article 1287 the assumption that the author of the inheritance and his/her heirs or legataries die all at the same time as a consequence of the same accident, or on the same date, and there may not be a form to find out who died first. The consequence of such assumption lies basically in the fact that there is no place then for any transmission of succession rights.

This figure of the simultaneous death must not be mistaken with another figure apparently similar, that is, the previous death of the assumed heir. By virtue of these last, the assumed heir dies before the death of the testator and, therefore, logically there can be no hereditary transmission.

III. Unworthiness to Succeed

166. The unworthiness to succeed may be a result from a series of causes specified in the Code. Certainly, Article 1313 already mentioned, specifically relates the lack of personality; crime; assumption of influence contrary to the freedom or the testator or the truth or integrity of the testament; lack of international reciprocity; public utility; and quitting or remotion of any charge conferred in the testament.

167. We have already explored that, according to Articles 22–24 CCDF, the capacity of physical persons is acquired by birth. However, even this date may claim to be retroactive at the moment of conception itself, and generates then a specific context of rights that include even the capacity to succeed once having certain notice of the conception at the time of death of the author of the inheritance. This rule, however, must be related to the effective viability of the newly born in which case it is necessary for him/her to remain alive for at least twenty-four hours or that he/she be presented alive to the civil registry.

It is clear that at the other extreme the person's death vanishes the juridical capacity.

168. It is convenient to warn that, as for foreigners, the capacity remains limited under the terms of Article 27, fr. I and Articles 32–33, of the CPEUM, that refer to the necessity that foreigners have to agree before the Federal Government (Secretaría de Relaciones Exteriores, SRE) in being considered as if they were nationals in respect to the goods that they pretend to acquire. In this way, foreigners cannot claim the protection of their national governments. It is expressly established that in a line of 100 km along the borders and of 50 km at beaches, foreigners can in no way acquire the dominion over lands and waters.

However, in view of that stated in Article 32 CPEUM, Mexicans must be preferred to foreigners in front of any sort of concessions, employment, charges, or commissions, as long as there is equity of circumstances and that it does not result in the indispensable quality of citizen. Article 33 CPEUM, according to a June 2011 reform, says that foreign people that do not possess Mexican nationality may not enjoy human rights that the Constitution recognizes. By the way, the Executive of the Union has the right to make all foreigners whose residence in the country is judged inconvenient, abandon the national territory or be deported.

169. The Foreign Investment Law (*Ley de Inversión Extranjera,* LIE, 1993), with important reforms in January 2014, was originally issued by the president Carlos Salinas de Gortari. This law prescribes the specific activities that foreigners may perform without permission from Mexican government. In any case the authorities, public notaries, public corridors and judges of the Civil Registry must demand from foreigners proof of their legal residence in the country, as well as the special permission in case to be required. As a matter of fact, Article 13 of LARCP says that foreigners can be ministries of any religious cult if their migration status is regular in terms of Migration Law. The LIE also establishes the proportion in which foreign capital may participate in our country, and the activities reserved in an exclusive way to the state and those others in which foreign investment may participate under specific amounts.

170. In case of crime the Civil Code enumerates a long series of possibilities of people becoming incapable to inherit either by will or statutory way, naming the following: Those people condemned by murdering the person of whose succession it is about, or his or hers parents, children, spouse or sisters; those people accusing of a crime that deserves capital punishers or prison, even when this accusation were founded, unless that act may have been precise for the accuser to save his life, his honour or that of his descendants, ascendants, brothers or spouse; the spouse adulterous, if it is about succeeding the innocent spouse; the coauthor of the adulterous spouse, either it is his succession or that of the innocent spouse; those people condemned for a crime that deserves penalty of prison, committed against the author of the inheritance, his children, his spouse, his ascendants or his brothers; the father and the mother in respect of the child exposed by themselves; the ascendants that may abandon, prostitute or corrupt their descendants; the other relatives of the author of the inheritance who, having obligation to feed him, may not have accomplished it; the relatives of the author of the inheritance who, being unable to work and without resources, may not have taken care of him in a charity establishment; whoever may use violence, deceit or fraud with a person for him to make, stop making, or revoke a will; whoever, according to the Penal Code, were guilty of suppression, substitution or supposition of infant, as long as it is referred to the inheritance that must have corresponded to this infant, or to the people related with such acts; and whoever may have been condemned for a crime against the author of the inheritance (Article 1316 CCDF).

171. The Code establishes a series of legal assumptions that limit in advance the capacity to succeed, and they refer to the presence of an influence directly opposite to the freedom of the author of the testament or the truth or integrity of the act. These legal assumptions will be analysed later on (*infra*, paragraph 173).

172. We have talked (*supra*, paragraph 168) about the limitation that foreigners may have in acquisition of goods in the matter that we are dealing with. It is interesting to state now that there is also incapacity to inherit in case of foreigners who according to the laws of their country of origin cannot transmit goods to Mexicans.

Such incapacity conforms a basic principle of international law that attends with justice the lack of reciprocity that sometimes may take place within the international ambit.

173. The existence of a valid cause of public utility conforms the next hypothesis of capacity to inherit, from a positive point of view. Certainly, such circumstances take place in relation to public establishments and private assistance institutions, because then the law protects the latter. Thus the law orders, for example, that donations, legacies, and bequest intended for private care in general, will be turned to a private assistance institution through the Private Assistance Board, according to that prescribed in Articles 24, 25 and 26 of the Institutions of Private Assistance Law of the Federal District (*Ley de Instituciones de Asistencia Privada para el Distrito Federal,* LIAPDF, 1988). The legal protection of these kind of institutions is such that it even takes the place of the eventual formality deficiencies.

However, such benefits are restricted as to how much they affect the capacity to inherit of religious associations, because in this case certain limitations are established for the assumption of influence contrary to the freedom of the testator, besides that the Secretary of State must resolve necessarily over the indispensable character of the landed property assets that are pretended to be inherited by any religious association according to Articles 15 and 17 LARCP.

174. Finally, the resignation or dismissal of some conferred charge in the testament defines the last cause of incapacity to inherit, because whoever may have refused, without any fair cause, the charge, or whoever may have been separated judicially of his/her exercise, cannot succeed in the goods (Articles 1331–1333).

§3. Succession Rules

I. The Classes of Heirs

175. Who has the right to inherit in the statutory way? In a general form, the law prescribes that those who inherit are the descendants, ascendants, spouses, relatives into the fourth degree and those who are living together as husband and wife, absolutely in this order. Only in case of the lack of the being mentioned, intervenes in the succession the public assistance, DIF (Article 1602, fr. II, CCDF).

In all of this there are two general principles in the Code. The first one refers to the rule of succession law that states that the closest relatives exclude the most distant ones. The second one establishes that all of those relatives that are in the same degree must inherit in equal parts.

However, it is necessary to take notice of a 1991 resolution which establishes in a precise form an exception to this principle, in relation to succession *per lineage*, by stating the following:

> It presents itself in a straight descending line, without limitation of degree, therefore, the son represents the father, if this one happens to die before the author of the inheritance; the grandson represents the grandfather, if both died before the *cujus*; even, the great-grandson may inherit also by lineage, when his direct ancestors have died; if several descendants attended instead of an ascendant who died before, all of them will inherit only the part of the dead ascendant before the author of the inheritance, that is, the lineage of the son who died before, will have the right to the share that corresponds to him; and finally, the inheritance *per lineage*, constitutes an exception to the principle that states that the closest relatives exclude the farthest ones.[99]

Nevertheless, the first principle implies the exception that distinguishes between the inheritance *per capita* and the inheritance *per lineage,* rule that is also applied being descendants or some collaterals of sons who died before, incapable to inherit, or that may have resigned to the inheritance (Articles 1609 and 1632).

Finally, it has already been said (*supra*, paragraph 137) that our law recognizes three kinds of parenthood. Well, then, in such a case, the parenthood of affinity does not give the right to inherit.

99. Bertha Celia Llamas Solís [1991] VII S.J.F. 438.

A. *Surviving Spouse*

176. The spouse may succeed in all of the deceased's assets under the condition that no other relative exists, either descendant, ascendant, or brethren (Article 1629).

So then, the first possibility is settled in the case that the spouse *supérstite* coincides with descendants. It is obvious that, in this case, such relatives necessarily set the spouse aside, specially if this one possesses goods. Let us suppose for a moment now that the widow or widower may not have any kind of goods – or else, that those he or she may have, do not match the part that corresponds to every child. If this is the case then the supérstite will have the right to a child, even if they were adopted.

If the spouse totally lacks goods, the *supérstite* must receive the portion in an integral form. If it is not so, the Code prescribes that, in justice, he must receive only the proportion that is lacking to match the individual portion of the coheirs.

The second possibility refers to the presence of the widow or widower with ascendants. In this case the Code confers half of the mass to the *supérstite,* and the other half to the ascendants.

Finally, the third possibility is that only the surviving spouse with brethren may survive, in which case the precept of the Code increments the portion in benefit of the widow or widower up to two thirds, of the whole of the mass conferring the remaining third to the brethren.

It must be clear now that as long as the *supérstite* attends with ascendants or with brethren, the rule that limits its portion to the former possession of own goods does not take place anymore.

B. *Descendants*

177. The succession of descendants is found to be regulated in the first term in the precepts of the Code. The general rule prescribes the children to divide everything into even parts, on the death of the parents.

Let us now suppose that there are ascendants. Well then, the rule remains the same: the children inherit everything and the ascendants are only protected in the case of aliments.

It has been said before that, at this point, a remarkable exception to the general principle of succession law is that the closest relatives exclude the farthest (Article 1604 CCDF), because in this case the descendants of ulterior degree inherit *per lineage.*

Quid iuris in the case of the adopted child? Certainly, the problem is not settled in the case of the plain adoption. In the simple adoption, however, there is a limitation that reduces the absence of the right to succeed between the adopted person and the relatives of the adoptant. The children in that case only have the right to eventual aliments.

C. *Ascendants*

178. It can be seen already in this context, that if there are only ascendants, these inherit even parts. Therefore, existing descendants and spouse will have the preference that the law grants them. The situation of adoptants should be mentioned here, because in this case there are two rules of particular application that state that in the case of adoptants with ascendants of the adopted by the simple method, the inheritance will have to be divided into even parts between the adoptant and the ascendants. On the other hand, if the spouse of the adopted attends with the adoptant, in this case the inheritance is divided into three even parts: two are given to the spouse, while the remaining third part is conferred to the adoptant.

D. *Collaterals*

179. The succession of collaterals represents the fourth derivation which the law recognizes in the case of statutory succession. It has been seen already how the law establishes a well organized succession system which is given even in mathematically opposite amounts.

The comparison of collaterals can only take place strictly in the absence of children, parents and spouse *supérstite*. Article 1630 states that in the case of exclusively brethren attending by both lines, all succeed in even parts. Now, if brethren attend with step brethren, the first inherits a double portion.

The situation aggravates when brethren attend with nephews, who are children of brethren or step brethren, who may have died before the own author of the inheritance, and that for any cause may not have been able to inherit (incapacity or resignation), because then brethren inherit – *per capita* – a double portion, and the nephews – *per lineage* – only once.

Let us see what happens in the hypothesis that there are no brethren. The law solves the problem by saying that children succeed, although the inheritance must be divided *per lineage* and each *lineage* must be divided *per capita*. We can imagine now the case in a more extreme situation: a radical absence of close relatives. Then any relative who is closest in the fourth degree will succeed. There is no distinction of line or double link and they inherit in even parts.[100]

E. *Concubines*

180. Finally, the new Articles 1368, fr. V and 1635 CCDF also appoint the concubine as having the right to inherit, comparing this subject to the succession of the

100. Almost all the codes of the Republic consider as legitimate heirs all collateral parents comprehended up to the fourth degree; however, the civil codes of the states of Guanajuato (Art. 2872), Oaxaca (Art. 1502), and Puebla (Art. 3360), include the collateral relatives up to the sixth degree.

spouse. The requirements are reduced to the cohabitation during two years immediately prior to death[101] or the simple fact of having procreated a child in common. The existence of several couples in the relationship voids automatically the right to inherit (compare Article 291*bis*–291*quintus*).

II. Representation

181. In Mexican law the figure of representation is provided for some cases of hereditary succession of collateral relatives. Indeed, the law prescribes that in the absence of descendants, ascendants, and spouse, brothers must inherit equally. However, law clarifies that if brothers come up with half brothers, the first ones will inherit a double portion.

Now, we should consider the case of brothers attending with other relatives such as nephews, or even attending with the children from brothers who have died, or from those who are unable, or from those who have renounced the inheritance. In all this cases the law says that those brothers will inherit *per capita*, and the other relatives *per lineage*.

If there are no more brothers, is clear that children will inherit. In this situation the inheritance must be divided *per lineage*, and a portion of each *lineage* must be divided *per capita*.

As we have told, law extends until the fourth degree (*supra*, note 103) the right to inherit. In this case relatives inherit in equal parts (Articles 1630–1634 CCDF).

III. Adoption

182. Let us deal now with succession rights that eventually correspond to the heirs involved in an adoptive relationship. We have already mentioned in different parts that the adoptant and adopted have a series of rights foreseen in the Civil Code.

Articles 293, 295, 410-D, 1612–1613 and 1620–1621 CCDF have a series of rules that prescribe the relationship of the adopted. Thus, the adopted inherits as a son in both kinds of successions; however, there is no right to succeed between the adopted and the relatives of the adoptant when the adoption is one of a simple kind –in some provincial codes. It is also important to clear up that the adoptant's parents –in a simple way adoption– have only the right to alimony when they attend with sons or other descendants of the adopted.

On the other hand, a situation may arise when adoptants might attend with the ascendants of the adopted –in a simple form–, in which case the inheritance of this last one must be divided into even parts. Let us suppose, finally, that the widow – or widower – of the adopted person comes together with the adoptants: The law

101. This term may be different according to local civil legislations. Thus, the CC of the states of Tlaxcala (Art. 2910), Quintana Roo (Art. 1534) and Tabasco (Art. 1698) demand the minimal term of a year's time; the CCGRO (Art. 1432) demands two, and the CCQRO (Art. 1497) and Veracruz (Art. 1568) demand three. In the rest of the national codes, the term is five years. The CCOAX does not prevent anything regarding this.

states that in this case, the inheritance is divided into three parts. One part will correspond to the adoptants, and the remaining two thirds, to the widow or widower, if such a case.

§4. The Rights of State on the *Bona Vacantia*

183. This hypothesis conforms a case of exceptional application in succession law. It is about the non-existence of surviving spouse, descendants, ascendants, collateral relatives and even *concubines,* all of which results in the succession of rights in favour of public assistance, through the System for the Family's Integral Development in Mexico City (Articles 1602, fr. II, 1636 and 1726 CCDF, and 843 CPCDF).[102]

102. Indeed, the State of Mexico foresees as a successor, in the absence of all of the callings in a statutory form, the State of Mexico's System for the Family's Integral Development; but in other provincial codes is appointed as a successor the public assistance –in general– or the tax office of the state (e.g., Art. 1569 CCVER).

However, it is worth noting that the CC of the states of Querétaro (Art. 1498), Puebla (Art. 3361) and Tlaxcala (Art. 2914) divide the inheritance giving a part to the public assistance, and even another to the local University. The CC of Guanajuato (Art. 2874) and Zacatecas (Art. 811) go beyond and designate exclusively the University as an heir, without any consideration to the public assistance.

On the other hand, the CC of Morelos (Art. 777 [cf. Art. 738 CFMOR]) and Sonora (Art. 1712) foresee as an heir the state – thus, in general – noting that a third part will be given to institutions of assistance, instruction, social or professional action, public or privately, established in the city of the deceased; another third part will be applied to similar institutions of general interest to the state, and the third part remaining will be destined to the state's public expenses. The alternative, if the mentioned institutions may not exist, is to divide also in three parts and to destine a part to the city public expenses of the domicile of the decedent and the rest to the state's public expenses. The state of Quintana Roo (Art. 1539) foresees the state, as the unique only successor, too.

Finally, if there is not more relatives, the State of Mexico foresees as a successor to the State of Mexico's System for the Family's Integral Development. The same case happens in Mexico City with the reforms made in June 2006.

Chapter 2. Testamentary Succession

184. The second remarkable line on the subject of successions in our civil legislation refers to the testamentary succession. Our Civil Code defines the will as 'a truly personal act, revocable and free, for which a capable person disposes of his goods and rights and declares or fulfils duties for after his death' (Article 1295).

The qualifier that the Code uses – even to a superlative degree – by saying 'truly personal' has settled some problems in practice. What happens, for example, when the notary appears at the domicile, and the testator dictates his will accompanied by his wife? Of course, it is quite clear that in the present situation, the prevention of Article 1295 CCDF is not being strictly fulfilled. However, an interesting sentence has resolved that 'There is no disposition that prohibits the spouse of the granter to be present during the making of the liberality, and no precept that may sanction that presence with the voidness of the testament.'[103]

This first chapter, which refers to wills in general, contains dispositions about the form to testate imposing, for example, the obligation to reduce the business to a strictly unilateral act. It is forbidden to make, thus, a testament of a reciprocal character, that is, where two people emit testamentary disposition each one in favour of the other or even both in favour of a third party (Article 1296).

Some other dispositions that impose limitations to the act of making a testament appear as well. It is said, for example, that the subsistence of the naming of the beneficiaries cannot be left to the free will of a third party, either as heirs, or as legataries. Such things cannot be done either with the portions that may eventually correspond to them. In any form, it is possible that this third party may have faculties to distribute the amounts or to choose the people who should be benefited, but this can only be made when the testator may have made the designation in a general form (Articles 1298–1299).

185. What happens if a testament is lost? This is a serious event that presents difficulties not easy to solve in practice. Of course, in any case it is necessary to precise the character of the lost will, because our Code offers, as will be seen, a plurality of forms to which the author of the will may appeal. Thus, if the will is found in the protocol of a notary public or registered in a public office, the problem is of course minor; but if the testament exists in a unique issue, then the interested parties will not be able to demand its accomplishment if they do not prove that the document is certainly lost or that it was stolen, the content of the document, and satisfy the legal formalities (Articles 1562, 1303 and 1549, CCDF).

§1. The Capacity to Make a Will

186. The capacity to make a will is necessarily assumed. Such is, certainly, the formulation contained in Article 1305, in a negative sense. However, it is obvious

103. Marco Antonio Irigoyen Sánchez [1973] LV S.J.F. 63.

that minors and the mentally stranded cannot have the capacity to make a will.[104] Thus, Article 1306 foresees: 'Incapable to make a will are the following: I. The minors who may not have become 16 years old yet, either men or women, and II. Those who habitually or accidentally do not have their integral judgment.' In this specific case, this precept derogates the general rule contained in Article 646 that defines the majority of age at 18 years.

187. The second case deserves deeper analysis. It is what the scientific doctrine certainly refers as the 'insane man' will, and in which provision the remaining Articles 1307–1312 are exhausted. For this, an interval of lucidity is required. It is required besides to make a written request addressed to the judge, who must immediately name two physicians to examine clinically the sick man. Then, after a formal act, and only if the recognition may certainly be favourable, it will proceed to the formation of the notarial will. Everybody must sign: the notary, the witnesses and the judge, as well as the sick man himself, if he is able to.

As it is seen, then, it is a very complex procedure that consists of two different formalities, that is, the judicial recognition, and the notarial formality.

The federal tribunals have pronounced on this. For example, let us imagine the case of a person who may be drunk and that, in those conditions, attends to make a will. In a sentence of 1967, the Supreme Court decided the following:

> Even admitting the state of drunkenness of the testator when he granted the will, is not necessarily deduced the total absence of his mental faculties that may make him incapable of making a will, when it was not demonstrated an absolute and complete degree of drunkenness, that may deprive him of his integral judgement.[105]

The expression used in Article 1306, fr. II of the CCDF also presents problems. It says that are incapable to make a will 'Those who habitually or accidentally do not have their integral (complete) judgment'. So, a federal sentence clarified that:

> The diction used in such a precept, without any scientific pretension, has a wide practical comprehension; and even when the term *cabal* is a synonym of the complete, just finished and exact and in such a sense it does not seem possible to predict the mental health that, as the physical, is rarely perfect; it is also understood for *cabal,* the normal. In this sense, undoubtedly, the law employs it referring to the act of making a will to reunite the proper requirements of a really true human act, characterized because it may be done with intelligence or knowledge of its meaning and of its reaches, and with a free will of wanting the aims of the act.[106]

---

104. Only the CC of the states of Quintana Roo (Art. 1252), Michoacan (Art. 479), Puebla (Art. 3065), Sinaloa (Art. 627, I), Tlaxcala (Art. 2641) and Tabasco (Art. 1386) point out an older age than fourteen to formulate a will, because in the rest of the country's civil legislation (e.g., the mentioned Art. 1306, CCDF) is demanded an age older than sixteen years for the exercise of that right.
105. Josefina Rocha de Saucedo and others [1967] CXVIII S.J.F. 114.
106. Guadalupe Gleason de Quiroz [1974] LXVII 65.

§2. Different Types of Wills

188. It has been said in advance that our civil codes have a great variety of testamentary forms. At the beginning, however, the will can only be classified into two large branches, which are, *ordinary* wills or *special* wills. The ordinary wills, as it is yet prescribed in the majority of our provincial codes, are the following: Open public will; Closed public will; Simplified public will; and Holograph will.

On the other hand, the special wills are reduced to the following: Private will; Military will; Mariner's will; and will done in a foreign country.[107]

The general norms for these eight kinds of wills are the following: first, it is established the people who are unable to act as witnesses: they are the *amanuenses* (scribes) of the notary; those minors under 16 years; those insane persons; those who do not understand the language that is spoken by the testator; the heirs or legatees, his descendants, ascendants, spouses or brethren; and those condemned by forgery (Article 1502). Nevertheless, the concurse as a witness of one of these persons only produces the voidness of the disposition that may benefit them.

189. In second place, the problem of who may be considered as *amanuense* is settled. It is the case of an archaic word, but utilized still in the juridical specialized language. This word, according to the *Diccionario de la Lengua Española*, means 'person who writes by dictation, writer' (from the Latin *amanuensis*). By the way, it must be mentioned here that the Civil Code of Tabasco of 1997 substitutes the word amanuense for 'auxiliaries' (Article 1573, fr. I).

Since 1965, a sentence of the federal tribunals decided a controversial case over the intervention of notarial office employees as witnesses according to that stated in Article 1502 fr. I, which mentions that the clerks of the notary cannot be witnesses to the will:

> When in an open public will it is demonstrated that the writer, is a person who takes down the dictation, employee, secretary or dependant of the notary, intervenes as an instrumental witness in the granting or an authorized testament by the own notary, they must be regarded to all legal effects as clerks … Consequently, if one of the witnesses that such precept refers to as clerks of the notary, it must be declared void and without effect the impugnated testament, even when that one may not have been typed or handwritten, but it must be

107. On classification of the kinds of testaments contained in the majority of the codes of the country, it is important to mention the following: the 2012 reforms in Mexico City (and in other same cases the 2002 reforms in the State of Mexico) have derogated the Closed public will, the Simplified public will, the Holograph wil, the Private will, the Military will and the Maritime will. Nevertheless this is not the case of the FCSIN, where the 2013 reforms have conserved the eight types of wills.

The CCQRO (Art. 1460*bis*) classify the will over *the housing of social or popular interest*, as well as the *aerial will* (Art. 1459). This last one is also consignated in the CCGRO (Art. 1381), where it is mentioned besides the *space will*. The CC of Aguascalientes, Oaxaca, Tlaxcala, and Puebla do not typify the holograph will. The CCNAY classify neither the maritime, nor abroad, nor military wills.

Finally, the CCVER (Art. 1454) names 'closed notarial will', to that which in other legislations is known as 'closed public' will and 'autograph' to the holograph will (Art. 1483). Both changes are purely a formality.

considered as such, as was duly stated, to the writer, copyist or employee or dependant of the notary and to whoever helps him in his general labors of the notary.[108]

190. In third place, another norm of general application is the one referred to the other characters that intervene in the formation of the will. For example, in the case of interpreters, which occurs when the testator ignores the corresponding language. In this case it is stipulated that the own testator has for himself/herself the right to name this intermediary.

The witnesses, not so long ago, resulted in indispensable presence – in the number of three – in the open public will. By virtue of an amendment (see *infra*, paragraph 191, note 110), this is no longer required, except in the case that the testator or even the own notary may request it, but even in this hypothesis the number is reduced to two.

To these witnesses, that still are necessary in other cases (closed public will, holograph, private, military, and maritime wills), are attributed mainly the functions of witnessing of knowledge of the testator, to make sure of his identity and to state his integral judgment and absence of co-action over his will (Article 1504).

The rules to identify the testator are very rigid. Precisely, Articles 1505–1506 express severity in the witnessing of this circumstance and they even demand, in case of doubt, the addition of all of the characteristic traces of the person, but in any case the testament does not have any worth until the identity of the author is not plainly justified.

At last, Article 1507 is strict as well in the provision to not leave blank sheets in the drawing up of a will.

191. The *open public will* receives the qualifiers of 'public' and 'open' due to the fact that it is given before an attester, that is, a public notary, for which it necessarily there is a register entry in the notarial protocol and, up to a very short time ago, recently it would be written, signed and authorized in the presence of three instrumental witnesses.[109]

This testamentary type demands the extensive intervention and follow-up of the notary, being responsible for this at all times for the writing of the clauses and of

108. Liselote Bondy Horak [1965] CI S.J.F. 127, 128.

109. Most of the codes of the Republic continue demanding the formality of the three instrumental witnesses at the moment of the granting of the act. By exception, the CC of the states of Nayarit (Art. 2647), Federal District (Art. 1513), Jalisco (Art. 2842), Baja California Sur (Art. 1418), Veracruz (Art. 1444), State of Mexico (Art. 1360), Queretaro (Art. 1388), Colima (Art. 1407), Sinaloa (Art. 832), and Sonora (Art. 1589) determine that, under request of the testator or of the notary, two witnesses will attend, but such requirement is merely optional.

In practice it happens that the act is done without the intervention of witnesses and, certainly, the dogmatic definition of the testament has remained reduced to the following: 'Open public will is the one that is granted before a notary', suppressing then the previous formula that would say: 'before notary and three witnesses' (e.g., Art. 1511 CCDF).

Coahuila (1999), Morelos (2006), Aguascalientes (2007) and Michoacan (2008) are still demanding even recently the presence of witnesses.

the strict adjustment with the will of its author, as well as the immediate latter reading, the imposition of the respective signatures, and the final authorization of the act.

Next, concrete dispositions of very specific application are the norm for the conduct of the responsible notary: Articles 1514 and 1516–1518 state the exceptional cases when the testator may not know or cannot sign, was entirely deaf, blind, or ignores the local language.

Finally, Article 1519 lists the principles of concentrated unity of the act and giving of attest of the notary in respect to the complete satisfaction of formalities, under punishment of inefficiency of will and serious responsibility to the notary.[110]

192. Diversely, in the provincial codes where yet admitted, the *closed public will* appear in no official protocol and for this reason it shows the character of 'closed'. However, it continues to be public because it involves the intervention of the notary and of witnesses.

It has already been seen that even when the person may not know or cannot write, sign or stamp a signature, this does not constitute any kind of impediment. However, there are other kinds of specific incapabilities that do constitute an obstacle to the formal expression of the testator. This is the case of the illiterate person, for example, or of those who do not know or cannot read, because these people are unable to make a closed will.

What happens, for example, if the author of the will is mute? In this case – and also in the case that person may just be deaf – the affected person may make a closed will, either by himself or herself, or asking some other person for help, but in any case, the person must sign a statement and sign it handwriting.

Let us now see what happens in the case of the deaf and mute. The provincial codes demand that the person with these disabilities must write, date and sign with the person own hand the whole document but demand, besides, that in the presentation act before the notary not only three, but five witnesses must attend, and once again the person must write, in the presence of all of them, the declaration that the pledge being dealt with contains his or her last will and is written and signed by this same person.

193. This closed public will may be written by the testator, but it can also be written by another person even using a common paper. The characteristic of this document is that immediately after being written, signed and firmed, it must be inserted in a closed envelope. Once this is done, he/she must exhibit it in the presence of three witnesses to the notary, declaring that his/her last will is contained in that paper. In this way, not even the attester notary can have the knowledge to know of the terms of the will. Neither can the witnesses know and the only possibility to know by a stranger lies in another person who must sign under petition of the author if he/she does not know or does not want to do it, and it is understood that this person has the entire trust of the author.

Thus, this testamentary modality satisfies entirely the requirement of confidentiality, not missing, instead its formal presentation before the notary. The notary must

---

110. As we will see next (*infra*, 194).

attest of the granting and must take care as well of the satisfaction of all formalities inherent to this kind of act. According to law, the notarial constancy must be extended to the cover of the document and once done, this must be signed by the testator, witnesses and notary.

The following step consists of delivering physically the will to the notary, on the part of the testator, the respective document, and then the notary must attribute in his/her protocol of the date when the testament resulted, authorized and returned to its author. This document may be kept by the testator, given to another person in his/her trust, or deposited in the judicial files.

It is interesting to note here an old sentence of the Supreme Court that refers to the great importance of the formalities in a closed public will. Thus, it is said that:

> The validness of the manifested will in the closed testament, makes itself depend on the scrupulous observance of the formalities the law appoints, and the lack of any of them is sanctioned with the deprival of effects of that will, that is, with the voiding of the testament, for which it is inadmissible that it must be more attended the substantiality of the testamentary disposition than to the external formalities of the document.[111]

194. Then, the notary is responsible for all the formalities contained in this legal chapter and therefore, as we said before, there are serious penalties against the notary in case of non-observance of such formalities. The Code states that the testament that may lack any of the formalities will not only remain ineffective, but the notary must also assume the entire responsibility for any damage and besides shall be penalized with loss of duty.[112] Even the breach of the routine written note of 'authorized' in the protocol of the notary – which irregularity does not transcend to the consequences of the act – in this case it carries the penalty of suspension to notary public for six months.[113]

If any person may have a closed will and may not report it, or else, may have suppressed it with bad faith, the person will fall under the penalties foreseen to that effect in the Penal Code and will also lose all right to inherit legitimately – if this is the case.

195. Some provincial codes refer yet to the *simplified public will* of the now repealed Article 1549*bis* CCDF. This Article said that a simplified public will is the one made immediately by the buyer in the same instrument that consignates the

111. Dolores Llera Guzmán [1958] XIII S.J.F. 356.
112. For example Aguascalientes, Art. 1432, and even the FC of Sinaloa, Art. 840, recently in 2013.
113. The codes of Guanajuato (Arts 2789 and 2775) and Quintana Roo (Arts 1464 and 1451) impose as well the sanction of loss of duty for the notary. In a similar case, the FCMOR (Art. 514) establishes the loss of duty for the notary too. Others, like those of Nayarit (Arts 2668 and 2654), Jalisco (Art. 2857), Baja California Sur (Arts 1438 and 1424) and Querétaro (Arts 1413 and 1397) make the notary respond only for the damages, besides the administrative sanction that may be imposed in the corresponding terms (this last one, only in the case of Nayarit), but they do not prevent the loss of employment (if it is certain that they consignate a penalty of suspension for six months in diverse hypothesis). The CCMICH (Art. 692) condemns only to the payment of damages and it does not consignate any case of suspension or lost of duty. The penalty rule is now derogated in Mexico City (e.g., Art. 1520, repealed in 2012).

acquisition, or defines the legal regularization, of a economically standard family house.[114]

However, this modality now in force in a few provincial codes,[115] is a novelty that is ostensibly set apart from the traditional Latin concept of will. It is now seen that the will is stated in the deed of acquisition or regularization, as if it were just another clause. It must also be drawn up by a notary public and it can be verified in a collective form, that is, that every coproprietory – if that is the case – may name heirs in respect to his/her portion. Admittedly, there is no impediment either allowing the spouse to intervene in the act, derogating then the banning disposition that we have already analysed before. However, it is expressly established that the heirs may claim directly the house, without any formality of inventory and without any granting of warranty.

Finally, the new notarial deed to the heirs is made in agreement with a specific, novel procedure. In view of this normative, it must be shown to the notary the certified copy of the act of defunction of the testator and the testimony of simplified public will. The notary will proceed to effectuate publications in the local newspapers with the data of the case and will gather as well from several offices, the facts relative to the existence of other wills. If there is no opposition, the notary will throw away the respective deed and will order its inscription in the Public Property's Register.

Whatever it may be, the final intention must be summarized in the fact that this form of a simplified will may solve, in an expeditious and economical way, the serious problems of titles and regularization of goods that are alike in our country, specially before the effort that is made by official dependences in charge to solve the problem in the administrative procedure.

196. The *holograph will* is known as well, in other codes, by the denomination of autograph will. This will must be totally hand written by the author and it must be done in a double copy, with a fingerprint on every issue, besides the signature. The original of the document must also be kept in a closed envelope and sealed so that it can be deposited in the Notaries' General Files (*Archivo General de Notarías*). The duplicate is utilized to put a note on the cover regarding delivery to the corresponding authority and already sealed is given back to the author.

The deposit in this office must be done personally by the testator, identifying in a plain form, and writing, as well with his/her bare hand, the respective declaration about the author and the contents of the document. Following this, the corresponding deposit will be formalized, including a written proof of receipt which will be

114. For example, in the State of Mexico the requirement regarding the amount is that the value of the real property may not exceed the amount of MXN 614,000 (USD 17,000 approximately). That is the equivalent to 25 times the daily minimum salary in force in the State of Mexico, raised to a year, in 2014.

115. This simplified public will is stipulated in the states of Nayarit (Art. 2683*bis*), Baja California Sur (Art. 1454), Chihuahua (Art. 1455), Querétaro (Art. 1460*bis*), Colima (Art. 1446*bis*), State of Mexico (Art. 1397*bis*), Sinaloa (Art. 870) and Sonora (Art. 1625*bis*). Among them, there are a few variations that may refer mainly to the maximum value of the real property.

noted in the registral files. Thus, the original must be kept under the direct responsibility of the person in charge. Anyway, the document may be retired at any time on the part of the testator.

If the holograph testament were made in a foreign country, the functionary who may have intervened in its deposit must remit it, by means of the Foreign Relations Secretary, to the Notaries' General Files, precisely within the term of ten days.

197. The *private will*, on the other hand, is allowed when the testator is attacked by a disease so violent and so serious that he does not have time for the notary to attend to make another type of will; or when there is no notary public or judge in the city; or when it may be impossible or very hard to attend the case; or finally, when militaries are in combat or become prisoners of war (e.g., Article 1498 CCVER).

It is an essential principle of this type of testament that the author may not be able to make a holograph will, because in another form, this last one has pre-eminence.

The private will must observe the following formalities: five reliable witnesses, or three in cases of extreme urgency, are required; the author will express his will free, writing down the document; next, the author and the witnesses will sign the will.

As is known, the private testament has an important limitation, that is, it can only be effective if the testator passes away precisely because of the disease or as a consequence of the danger he/she was in. If this is not the case, the testament becomes void if the author is still alive one month after cessation of the cause of emergency.

According to law, the witnesses must describe in detail the place, time, day, month, and year when the will was granted; if the testator was fully recognized, heard and seen by the witnesses; the tenor of the disposition; if the testator was in his integral judgment and free of any force; the reason why the private will was granted; and if they know that the testator died or not because of the disease or the danger in which he was (e.g., Article 1507 CCVER).

However, such witnesses declaration will only take place once the author's death has occurred. The declarations will serve as a basis for the judicial decree about the will.

Under these circumstances, the briefing of the term in which the author's death must be produced in relation to the date of granting of the will, makes the latter reception of the declarations easier to obtain. But even in this case it is necessary to suppose that any of the witnesses may have died or are absent. There are specific dispositions regarding these problems. So, there must be always a minimum of three very reliable and in agreement witnesses. In case of a witness is in another city, this witness will be examined by a local judge.

198. The *military will* requires another very specific formality. As its denomination indicates, it can only be carried out by military personnel – or assimilated to the Army – in circumstances of military attack. However, the simple condition of prisoner of war is assimilated to this circumstance, even without imminent danger.

In these cases, the legislation allows the simple declaration of will before two witnesses, either in a direct form, or delivering them in a closed paper, with a bare signature of the author. The high officials have the obligation to deliver the document thus composed to the National Defence Secretary. Also in cases of nuncupative will, the witnesses of the act and the high officials will inform to the competent authority.

Also applicable to this military will are the dispositions about the necessity of latter witnesses declaration and judicial decree about the will.

199. Under similar conditions, the *maritime will* may be written in the presence of two witnesses and of the captain of the navy, as long as the author is on the open sea on board a ship. Such will must be made in duplicate and the captain must write an explicit entry in the ship's logbook.

Upon arrival in port, the captain must deposit before the corresponding functionaries the document concerned with a duplicate of the entry in his or her logbook. For safety reasons the ship's captain must demand a receipt of the delivery and make note of this in the logbook.

Meanwhile, the functionaries who receive the document must proceed to sent it to the Foreign Relations Secretary. This Secretary will command the publication of the document as soon as he/she is informed of the death of the author.

Also applicable, finally, to this maritime will is the provision that the decedent may die out at sea or within a month starting from the date of landing at a place where the person may have been able to ratify or grant, once again, this last disposition.

200. Finally, our CCDF briefly refers in Articles 1593 and 1594, the *will made abroad*. If this is the case, it is clear that the will must observe the form in force in the local law. In this case the Mexican functionaries with official representation in that place, will have the character of notaries according to Article 44, fr. IV of the Mexican Foreign Service Act. They have the obligation to remit an authorized copy to the Foreign Relations Secretary, where the procedure to elaborate an act of delivery and to proceed to the publishing of the news of the testator's death, must be followed.[116,117]

---

116. Talking on wills, they have been produced some accelerated changes. One of them has to do with the implementation of the programmes 'September, month of the testament' and 'Hereda' ('Inherit'). The first programme has been issued in 2004 and since then, were made over 4 million registered wills in all over the country. The notaries fees were fixed to the 50% from what was established in the ordinary rate (USD 200) and only with the requirement of certifying to be the owner of the goods and showing an official identification. The second one, the popular agrarian programme 'Hereda', has made possible the elaboration of more than 600,000 instruments since 2000. The programme has given multiple benefits to the families of country people, livestock farmers, and rural entrepreneurs.

It has to be mentioned here the notable effort taken by the government of the state of Veracruz with the named *economic wills*, which facilitate to grant acts of last will to humble people who are elders (being older than sixty years), and the exemption of tax payment (for legal notice in the Notaries' General Files), the whole for an amount to pay of just USD 60.

117. On the other hand, it was issued the Law of Anticipated Will (*Ley de Voluntad Anticipada*) for the Federal District (*Gaceta Oficial*, 7 Jan. 2008). This new law try to prevent the so-called 'medical obstinacy' to maintain alive a person. The document of 'anticipated will' has to be validated by a notary public or in an alternative way by health authorities and two witnesses.

In this same matter, at the end of November 2008 the General Health Law was reformed, making appear the Eighth Title *bis* 'On the palliative cares to the sick persons in a terminal situation', in

§3. The Joint Will

201. By expressed disposition of our Code (Article 1296), it is clearly established that two or more people cannot testate in the same document. This is, of course, a reasonable consequence of the truly personal attribute that is found in the rigorous definition of the will (Article 1295).

This impossibility to make a joint will is absolute, because it cannot be done in any case, either in favour of a third alien party or to a reciprocal advantage. This last case comprehends as well the impossibility that a spouse makes a joint will in favour of the other and the other way around, in the same act. Obviously, this possibility may be legally given only in case where each one makes a will, in separated acts.

In any case, it is clear that an important exception, expressly foreseen in some provincial civil codes, is defined in the simplified public will that has already been an object of analysis (*supra*, paragraph 195).

§4. Revocation of a Will

202. The possibility of revocation is an essential characteristic of a will. Certainly, considering that the testament is a truly personal act and, by definition, absolutely revocable and free (Article 1295, *supra*, paragraph 184), it is plain to see that it can be revoked at all times, even without the necessity of a specific cause or ulterior motive. Thus, Article 1493 states that 'the resignation of the faculty to revoke the will is void'.

In fact, the prior testament is revoked automatically by another latter one, even without an expressed declaration of the author (Article 1494). There is only one exception, that confirms precisely the free will of its author, that is, that the testator expressly clarifies his/her will regarding the other original will which subsides, either in a total form, or in a partial one.

However, this general principle of the revocation of the wills concerns with problems that legislation had to solve. Certainly, what may happen if the second will results expired by incapacity or by resignation of the beneficiaries? Article 1495 expressly prevents the prior testament to be revoked anyway.

203. A similar figure to the revocation of the wills is the expiration dead. The expiration date does not suppose, as in the former case, the intervention of the

---

virtue of which it is included the integral care to preserve the quality of patient's life through the prevention, treatment, pain control, and other physical and emotional symptoms. According to this law, the sick patient in terminal situation has the right to the volunteer suspension of the cure treatment, and the beginning of the strictly palliative treatment, that is to say, focused on the exclusive manner to the diminution of the patient pain or discomfort (Art. 166*bis,* 6).

Finally, it has been proposed the creation of the figure of *inverse mortgage*, which is oriented to benefit old adults (being older than sixty years) or different capacities people. This particular mortgage consists in a guaranteed credit through a house, and allow the favoured person to obtain a rent for life.

expressed will of the author to declare the original will void. Certainly, the expiration date involves a different group of causes that refer specifically to the following aspects, according to Article 1497:

The testamentary dispositions expire and remain void, relative to heirs and legataries:

(i) if the heir or legatary dies before the testator or before the accomplishment of the conditions on which the inheritance or legacy depend;
(ii) if the heir or legatary become incapable to receive the inheritance or legacy; and
(iii) if he gives up his right.

There is however an important exception. Such hypothesis is found in Article 1498 that refers to the absence of expiration date in the case that the will may contain any relative fact that conditions its efficiency to an unexpected event. In this case the testament subsists in its terms, although the news of the fact is known even after the beneficiary's death. Certainly, the non-acquired rights by the direct beneficiary must be transmitted directly in this case to the respective heirs.

§5. Provisions in a Will

204. As the will constitutes a truly personal act and is, by essence, revocable and made with entire freedom, where it is usually covered by the entire patrimonial mass that a person has proprietary over, its preparation often involves improvisational consequences that the normative of the Code tries to anticipate. Chapter IV of Title II of Book III consists of a total of twenty-four articles and it is denominated 'On the conditions that may be put down in the wills.'

As a general principle, the fact that a person is entirely free to establish the conditions which he or she may wish to dispose of his or her goods, is ratified in Article 1344.

The Civil Code regulates in a general form the different kinds of obligations in Articles 1938–2028, under the title that refers to 'Modalities of obligations'. Such a dogmatic scheme must serve as a guide to interpretation and supplementary application under the specific testamentary conditions. In fact, Article 1345 establishes that the conditions so regulated in this last section must be foreseen by the general rules established in Articles 1938–1960.

205. In the specific testamentary dispositions, the Civil Code regulates a number of modalities. The first ones are the named *conditional dispositions*. They refer to the voiding or inefficiency of certain conditions that cannot comply with the testamentary disposition. Thus, the condition that may result as physically or legally impossible to give or to do, voids the institution. The condition that the heir or the legatary make at the same time, another testament setting their expected benefits in favour of the original testator or somebody else, is also prohibited. In this same sense, the negative conditions that impose the prescription of not giving or not doing, are equally not set. It is the same case with reference to the obligation of not refuting the testamentary disposition, under the penalty of loss of related goods or benefits (Articles 1347, 1349 and 1355). Finally, the obligatory condition that may be imposed on the heir or legatary relates to the fact of being married or not, is also part of this group of prohibitions, because such condition will be regarded as unset (Article 1358).

The second ones are named *term (or time) dispositions*. Let us suppose that the testator may impose a condition that suspends, for a short time, the execution of the will. In this case the heir acquires the right anyway and, therefore, transmits it to his/her heirs.

There is another related rule when a specific disposition has been stipulated, a term for its exercise which may not be imposed. In this case, the legated object will remain under the power of the executor and this person always remains responsible for the accomplishment of the condition, which must be satisfied before the delivery. The same happens when some duty in the testamentary disposition may have been stipulated.

Other legal precepts related with the term dispositions have to do with the legacy that consists in periodical benefits, either known or not with certainty the date when they start or the date when they must finish (Articles 1363–1367).

What happens if the condition imposed cannot be satisfied? In this case a double situation has to be distinguished: the first possibility refers to the fact that the beneficiary may have unfruitfully done all that was in his or her power for its completion. If this were not so, the lack of accomplishment of the condition must not affect the heir and indeed, that is the sense of Article 1346.

Let us now look at the second possibility, that is, the one which refers to the fact that the beneficiary may not have plenty occupied in gathering the requirements. In this case, it is of course unfair to effect the transmission; the condition must be regarded as not accomplished and therefore, the corresponding right is not generated.

§6. Restrictions

206. Even when our guide continues to be the principle of freedom of the will dispositions (Articles 1295 and 1344 CCDF), it is clear anyway that the philosophy of the Civil Code maintains a scheme of a certain restriction that limits, in some cases, the absolute freedom of the testator.

These restrictions may be appreciated quite clearly in the case of the preservation of freedom to testate one's own successors. Thus, the substitution of heirs or legataries that comprehend more than a life generation is absolutely prohibited. Also it is void the conditional disposition on a heir about not being able to alienate certain estate goods. It is also unlawful the denominated *fideicomisaria* disposition, that is to say, the disposition for the anticipated and forced substitution of the heir at the moment of decedent's death (see Articles 1473 et seq.). It is also prohibited, of course, the condition that may be illegal. For example, the condition imposed to the successor to get married – or not to get married – will be disregarded, because illegal.

I. The Legitim

207. In our juridical system the institution of the legitim does not exist as it does, for example, in Spanish law, which constitutes forced heirs by two parties and it only leaves the free disposition of the third remaining party (Articles 806–808 CCESP). However, it is true that in the past this system operated in the Mexican Civil Code of 1870. By modifying this legislation in 1874, the institution of the legitim was abandoned and the system passed to the present legislation with absolute freedom to make a will.

II. Maintenance Provisions

208. Another important series of restrictions refer to maintenance provisions (Article 1368). Indeed, the testator must provide *children support* to those descendants under 18 years in respect of which he may have a legal obligation; to the descendants that are incapacitated to work; duty of alimony to the spouse *supérstite* when is incapacitated to work and may not have enough goods;[118] maintenance provision to the ascendants; to the concubine, in certain cases;[119] and finally, to other collateral relatives into the fourth degree in certain cases, too (Article 1368).[120]

These restrictive dispositions of testamentary freedom are just in case of impossibility of relatives closest in degree. For this reason, the testator must relate in the will the people who, according to this disposition, have the direct obligation to satisfy the need by their proximity in the relationship.

Along with this rule it is necessary to mention another important benefit. It consists that the right to be fed is only generated by the people who may not have goods; but it may be that even having goods, the economic proportion does not match the pension that should correspond to them. So, in this case the testator must pay the difference.

However, it is clear that the right to be fed is generated only when the extremes are reunited, of any of the causes foreseen in Article 1368 aforesaid. But another two important restrictions must be added. In first place, the eventuality that the maintenance creditor is guilty of bad behaviour; in second place, the eventuality that according to the provision contained in Article 1370, acquire new goods. In both cases, the maintenance obligation ceases, of course.

In counterpart, it is clear that this right to maintenance is not quittable or negotiable (Article 321).

209. What happens if the mass of the inheritance is not enough to cover all of the legal maintenance provisions? In this case, the law provides a careful series of

---

118. In the case of the spouse *supérstite* the alimony obligation will only subsist as long as he/she does not get married and 'lives honestly', except another expressed disposition of the testator.
119. Similarly, in the case of concubine, this right will only subsist while the person does not get married and observes 'good behavior'. If the testator lived with several people as if they were his spouses, none of them will have the alimony.
120. In the case of collaterals relatives, the obligation will only subsist if they are handicapped, or as long as they are not eighteen years of age, if they do not have goods to solve their necessities.

priorities, because if the hereditary property is not enough to feed all of the people mentioned in Article 1368, the descendants and the spouse *supérstite* will be treated in an even distribution; then, the ascendants will be paid in a proportional way; later on, the brothers and the concubine; and finally, the other collateral relatives into the fourth degree – all of them will be also treated in a proportional distribution – (Article 1373).

210. Now, it is interesting to refer here to the consequences of the non-observance of the maintenance obligation. The Civil Code says that the testamentary disposition results without effect, and with this it means that the will benefits must precisely be reduced in a proportion equal to the alimentary assignation not covered. Thus, those left out have only the right to be granted the pension that should have been paid, but the testament continues intact in all of the rest, according to the general principle of law *utile per inutile non vitiatur* (Article 2238).

It is important to discuss here an interesting case solved by the Supreme Court that refers to the non-efficacy of the testament in which the *supérstite* spouse is not instituted as an heir and is not left any maintenance provisions either. Our highest tribunal has solved its non-efficacy pleading the following:

> Not having any transcendence (against the right that the plaintiff in the circumstance) that the spouse may have stopped living in the house where the author of the inheritance may have lived and where the will was granted, because there is no disposition that may affect her legally.[121]

Finally, at the end of these dispositions that refer to the maintenance provisions, Article 1376 mentions that this obligation is under the charge of the author of the inheritance and it results at the end burden of the whole hereditary mass that is being transmitted. The only exception takes place when the testator charges any of the heirs with some specific maintenance provision.

§7. Interpretation of a Will

211. The general rules of interpretation are found contained in Articles 1851–1857 CCDF, within the frame of the general theory of contracts. The relative provisions to the clarification of the terms of a will are so specific that the legislator has referred to them in two different places, although there is no special chapter about interpretation. Certainly, the legislator foresees norms concerning the matter in Articles 1300–1304 (about 'Wills in general') and, of course, in Articles 1381–1390 (about 'Heirs').[122]

In Article 1300 it is foreseen that if a testamentary disposition is not clear (when it is said for example: 'I appoint my relatives as my heirs or legataries'), then it must be understood that such designation refers to the closest relatives. In order to decide

121. María Antolín Barajas Vda. de Villalpando [1959] XXIX S.J.F. 253.

122. The CC of the State of Jalisco establishes a detailed regulation in Arts 2671–2673, stipulating the rules of interpretation of this kind of act.

who these 'closest relatives' are, attention must be paid to the order of statutory succession that is found in Articles 1599 et seq.

In any case, the essential principle in the matter of wills is that all testamentary clauses must be treated in the literal sense and this rule does nothing but repeat the terms of Article 1851, where it is stated that the literal sense of clauses must be followed. Such rule has the following exception: if it appears that evidently it was another testator's will, then the rule is abandoned, regarding this manifest intention of the testator.

Now then, to regulate in its proper terms this inquiry on the testator's will, it must be recurred of course to the integral context of the expressed will. The Code prescribes that auxiliary proof may be surrendered on the part interested.

212. Let us now analyse briefly the reference to the testamentary cause. Our Code does not recognize the cause as an element of the contracts (compare Articles 1794–1795). It even, when there is need to refer to it, employs deliberately the expression *motif* or *objective* of the contracts (Article 1831). However, in certain dispositions – precisely in Articles 1301 and 1304 – the legislator takes into account the expression of cause for the necessary interpretation.

Certainly, if the cause expressed in the will is finally mistaken and has determined the author's will, such dispositions cannot have any effect. However, if the testator has expressed literally a cause that although true, may be illegal, such clause will be regarded as not written at all.

When the testator institutes the heirs without a designation of which is their part, it must be understood that they will inherit in even parts.

Chapter 3. Acts *Inter Vivos* Related to the Estate

§1. Estate Planning

213. It is true that future things may be object of contracting, but it is comprehensible that for moral reasons it cannot be the inheritance of a living person, even when this person gives his/her consent (Article 1826 CCDF).

Indeed, immoral reasons may provoke the beneficiary to wish the death of the person whose inheritance deal was negotiated. Besides, there is another reason as well, that interests the traffic of goods, because the State cannot authorize such negotiations to be carried out and its execution must wait until the uncertain date of decease.

The succession rights can be transmitted, however, with a detailed expression of the goods that form part of the hereditary common property if the partition has already been made, or else, without numbering the things that form part of the portion. The Code prescribes that in this last case the transferor is only obliged to respond to his or her legitimate quality of heir, but then he/she is not obliged to respond to the eventual liens or encumbrances upon the properties of the parties that compound its portion (Article 2047).

The explanation of these dispositions resides in the fact that the beneficiaries acquire their right to all of the mass as a common patrimony, that is, all of them are beneficiaries.

This precept must be related with the Article 1289 which prescribes that the heir may, certainly, dispose of his/her right, but he/she will not be able to dispose of the concrete objects of his/her portion until the partition is effectuated. It is understood that the death of the author must have occurred as prescribed in Article 1291, that recalls then the provisions of Article 1826.

214. With respect to the *procedure* that must be observed in the transmission of succession rights, the obligation to notify the coheir for the use of the right for the preferential transmission is imposed.

The notification must take place under certain formalities that the Code reduces to the judicial form, or intervention of notary public, or by means of two witnesses. Choosing any of these three forms, the heir must make known the sales' conditions and he is obliged to await for a term of eight days the eventual replay of the coheirs.

In the event that any of the coheirs may respond in a positive form, the seller only has the remedy of effectuating the sale in favour of this one, precisely according to the proposed conditions, setting aside then any other stranger.

The consequences of the omission are rather serious, because the Code states clearly (Article 1292 *in fine*) that in any other way the sale is void. It is also certain that only for the passing of time without an answer from the coheir, is the right for the preferential transmission lost. So, the seller might be found again in legitimate conditions to effectuate the sale.

What happens if two or more coheirs may wish to make use of this preferential right? As it is difficult to make a fair decision in this case in view of the equality of characteristics, the Code has set up the preference for whoever may represent a major portion in the inheritance. It cannot be said that this solution may be really fair, because there are even reasons, in a contrary sense, to back up the pretension of whoever has less. Finally, *quid iuris* if both parts are even? Then the Code, unable to decide, appeals to luck (e.g., tossing a coin!).

It is clear that if the alienation of the hereditary goods is made to a coheir, no application has the right of preference foreseen in Article 1292. In this case then it attends the manifest preference of the seller.

§2. Donations

215. In our law system, donations (gifts) constitute a diverse contractual kind which are considerably set apart from succession law. Even systematic placement of the institution is very far apart from what corresponds to succession law. Regarding donations, Title IV of the Second Part of Book IV refers mainly to 'Obligations in general', and next specifically to 'Diverse kinds of contracts'. Thus, the contract of donation is marked with the number four in a series that starts from the promise of contract – or preparatory contract – goes on to the sales, continues briefly to barter, and ends up with gifts and mutual loans, all of them, except the first – promise of contract–, forms of dominion transmission.

In terms of Article 2332, donation is a contract by which a person transfers to another, freely, a part or the totality of his present goods. However, it is expressly stated that these donations can only take place between living people and thus (Article 2339) donations made after the death of the donor come under the norms of succession law that we have already studied. The same is decided in the case of donations between fiancées and between spouses, because they come under the special regime foreseen in Articles 232–234 and Articles 219–231 respectively, that have already been an object of analysis.

§3. Trusts

216. Diversely, our legislation applies an approximately similar institution to the figure of the Anglo-Saxon *trust,* this time in a completely separate legislation from the civil law. Thus, the General Law of Securities and Credit Operations (*Ley General de Títulos y Operaciones de Crédito*, LGTOC, 1932) foresees in its Articles 381–407 the specific rules of operation of the *fideicomiso.*

At present there is no controversy about the historical origin of the *fideicomiso* anymore. In fact, a federal sentence from 1970 has stated already in unquestionable terms the fact that:

> As a rather peculiar business different to other businesses, the 'fideicomiso' appears regulated in the Mexican legislation in 1932, when the LGTOC came into force. Formerly, it was introduced in the Institutions Credit Law from 1924, which made a reference to it without any regulation, and the law over the same matter, from 1926, considered *fideicomiso* it as an irrevocable

> command. Its immediate predecessor is the North American trust, whose obligation in a juridical aspect has been defined as an obligation of equity.[123]

The Mexican scientific doctrine has characterized this business in the following terms: 'Contract by means of which a physical person or a moral one transfers the property over part of his goods to a trust institution, for a licit aim, that the person himself appoint in the respective contract.'[124] However, the LGTOC says in its Article 381 that in virtue of this business, a person who is nominated as *fideicomitente*, devotes certain goods to a licit, specific object. This contract is addressed precisely to a financial institution that then receives the name of *fiduciaria*. The person who receives the benefits of this business is called *fideicomisario*.

The *fideicomisario* may be a physical person, or a juridical one; it can also fall on one or several people, either in a simultaneous form or in a successive one.

217. What can we say about the juridical nature of *fideicomiso*? The Mexican doctrine has supported, in a first interpretation, that *fideicomiso* is a fiduciary business; a second interpretation, however, conceives it as unilateral act, in virtue of which the *fideicomitente* establishes his or her will and the object of the business. Diversely, Rodolfo Batiza[125] express his opinion by considering *fideicomiso* as a contract and, even more, as a bilateral perfect reciprocal contract.

On the other hand, Domínguez Martínez devotes a wide space to the treatment of the problem analysing even its historical origins and the diverse doctrines that have been used concerning the matter. He finally pronounces his opinion in the following sense:

> *Fideicomiso* is a juridical business that is constituted by means of the unilateral will of a subject called fiduciaria, in virtue of which, this one destines certain goods or rights to a licit and determined aim, and the execution of the acts that may tend to the achievement of that aim, must be done by the fiduciary institution that may have been obliged contractually to it.[126]

Diversely, some sentences of the federal tribunals have stated the following:

> There is a such a great difference between the civil property and the fiduciary titularity, because in the first case it had the faculty to have and make use of a good, only with the modalities and limitations that laws may fix; in exchange, in the second the bearer does not have the right to have the good, because he cannot make use of it for its advantage of the possession and of the yieldings.[127]

123. Elvira Razcón de Macín and others [1970] XXI S.J.F. 39.
124. M. Acosta R., 'Fideicomiso', in *Diccionario Jurídico Mexicano*, Instituto de Investigaciones Jurídicas (Mexico: UNAM-Porrúa, 1989), 1441 et seq.
125. R. Batiza, *El Fideicomiso, Teoría y Práctica*, 4th edn (Mexico: Porrúa, 1980), 135.
126. J.A. Domínguez M., *El Fideicomiso*, 6th edn (Mexico: Porrúa, 1996), 188.
127. María de los Dolores Teresa Saldívar Porras et al. [1980] CXXIX S.J.F. 53.

> Fideicomiso, then, is a contract in which goods are found destined to the final aim of the business and the representation in defense of the interests corresponds to the fiduciary ... because of it, it is wrong that it may be in presence of a society or moral person, because the fideicomiso is a contract and being so, it cannot be considered as a juridical collective person.[128]

The *fideicomiso* must be stated in a written form. It is clear that in some cases the public formality of the notarial instrument will be required – if it is about real property. Even the solemn form will be required – if it is the case of a testamentary disposition. Besides all that, it must be taken into account the inscription in the Public Registry of Property to be effective against third parties.

218. There are some specific limitations in the contract of *fideicomiso.* Article 394 LGTOC says expressly that secret *fideicomisos* are forbidden; also, those that may concede benefits to diverse people in a successive form according to their death – unless all they are living or conceived at the moment of the *fideicomitente*s' death – and in like manner those *fideicomisos* which are older than fifty years, except that it may concern public institutions, or beneficence institutions. In terms of law, the *fideicomiso* may be extinguished by reaching aims; for becoming the accomplishment of the suspensive condition that it may depend on impossible, or for not having been verified in the designated term or, not being that, into the term of twenty years following its constitution; by having fulfilled a resolute condition that *fideicomiso* may have been subjected to; by an expressed agreement between the interested parties; by revocation done by the *fideicomitente* when this may have reserved expressly that right for himself in the case of *fideicomisos* created over third-party fraud; and even for non-payment of fiduciaria fees.

Once *fideicomiso is* extinguished, it is clear that the goods or rights destined for this purpose must return to the *fideicomitente* or *fideicomisario,* according to contract. No public form is required in this act, even being about real property, because it is enough to make an entry in the initial constitutive document, with the corresponding inscription in the Public Registry of Property.

§4. Insurance Contracts

219. Applicable in this case is a specific normative as well. Certainly, the Law Concerning Insurance Contracts (*Ley sobre el Contrato de Seguro*, LCS, 1934) expressly regulates this kind of contract, defined in Article 1st: 'By a contract of insurance, the insurance company obliges itself, by means of a bonus, to compensate a harm or to pay an amount of money by being verified the eventuality foreseen in the contract.'

It is important to say, however, that sea insurance and social insurance are subjected to other diverse laws, that is, Navigation and Maritime Trade Law (*Ley de Navegacion y Comercio Marítimos*, LNCM, 2006), Articles 186–253, and Social Insurance Law (*Ley del Seguro Social*, LSS,1995).

128. Nacional Financiera, S.N.C. [1995] XV S.J.F. 187.

However, Article 7, reformed in 2013, refers to the general conditions of the insurance, precisely about the formulations of offers drawn by the insurance companies. This precept must be related to the diverse Article 24 that demands easily legible characters in favour of the customer for the policy, as well as in the additional documents, that is, individual certifications of group insurance, open policies, provisional certificates, covering notes, etc.

The most important document is, of course, the policy. Articles 19–30 command that for the formality of this document the insurance contract must be stated necessarily in a written form. Except for the confessional proof, no other proof will be admissible to prove its existence. This policy must contain the names and addresses of the contracting people, and the signature of the insurance company; the designation of the insurance person or thing; the nature of the guaranteed risks; the starting moment from which the risk and endurance is guaranteed; the amount of the guarantee; the fee or insurance bonus; the specific mention that it is a obligatory insurance in terms of Article 150*bis*; and other clauses that legally be set in the policy, according to law; as well as the legally agreed by the contracting people (Article 20).

It is also important to note, concerning the perfection of the contract of insurance, that the theory of the information (Article 21, LCS) is followed, breaking thus the general rule of the Civil Code (Article 1807, CCDF) and of Commercial Code (Article 80)[129] that establish the perfection of the contracts among absents in the reception stage. Thus, Article 21 says that the insurance contract is perfected from the moment when the proposer may be acquainted with the acceptation of the offer.

The client may ask for the corresponding rectification of the policy in the event of an error or discrepancy. But this rectification must be requested precisely within the term of thirty days following the reception of the policy. If the term expires without any request, the stipulations will be understood as accepted. For a longer guarantee of the consumer, Article 25 of LCS, which contains this disposition, must be inserted textually in the document.

However, it is expressly commanded that the bonus must be paid in the customer's domicile, unless there is an expressed agreement to the contrary. As it is obvious, the bonus expires at the moment the contract is withheld with reference to the first period, according to the unit of bonus chosen.

The specific contracts of insurance foreseen in this law are the contract of insurance against fires, insurance over expected profits, insurance over cattle, insurance over ground transportation, insurance against responsibility, and insurance over bail.

Finally, all of the actions that are derived from an insurance contract will expire precisely within a two-year term, counted from the date of the event that gave origin to it, except in the case of death in life insurances (five years). Any commitment to the contrary is void (Articles 81 and 83, LCS). All of the dispositions of this law, actually, have the character of imperativeness and therefore do not admit any pact to the contrary, unless it is thus expressly established.

129. According to a reformation of May 2000.

§5. OTHERS

220. An approximately similar concept may be found in the *contract of life interest* that our Code foresees in Articles 2774–2791 (CCDF), established in this case as a species of random contracts of which gambling, betting and buying of a expected future thing, also take part.

In virtue of the contract of life interest, 'The debtor obliges himself to pay a pension periodically during the life of one or more determined people, by means of the delivery of an amount of money, or a movable good, or real estate appraised, whose dominion is transferred immediately' (Article 2774).

As it has been seen, this kind of contract is made *inter vivos* and may be constituted through a donation or through a testament, and in these two cases it is clear that it adopts a free will character.

The fundamental characteristics of this contract lies, in the first place, in its character at random, because it is not known what the fringe benefits are which must be finally covered during the entire life of the contract. In the second place, in the fact that it is about a contract that transmits effectively the dominion of the object of the contract, whether money, a movable good or a real estate. Finally, in the third place, one of the most distinctive characteristics of this negotiable form lies in the fact that it is constituted over the period of life of a determined person – or several – over whose subsistence, brief or prolonged, depends on the duration of the contract.

The juridical effects of this contract are typical as well: the property or the goods are transmitted immediately and then obligations and rights emerge simultaneously. Thus, the owner of the interest delivers the money or the thing immediately and then he/she is obliged to guarantee the necessary conditions for the execution of that agreed on.

However, the person who has received the object and who performs now as the single owner, starts its condition of debtor obliged to pay the corresponding pension periodically as was previously agreed on. This is a fundamental obligation.

But let us see what happens if the pensions are not punctually paid. In this case, Article 2782 CCDF states that even this non-fulfilment does not give the faculty to the pensioner for him/her to demand the reimbursement of the capital or the devolution of the object and he/she has only the right to demand of the debtor solely the payment of the expired ones, asking exclusively for the insurance of those that are just about to expire. The doctrine points out that this constitutes a clear exception to the general rule foreseen in Article 1949 about the implicit faculty of solving the obligations with reciprocal rights and duties, when one of the parties may not accomplish the corresponding duties.

Finally, it is clear that the beneficiary pensioner has the right to be paid the pension that was agreed. Of course, this obligation of payment depends precisely on the subsistence of the person or people elected, for which it is on them the obligation to demonstrate the survival of the corresponding person (even about himself or herself [Articles 2788 et seq.]).

The contract formality is the written one, as is expressly foreseen by Article 2776. However, when it is about real property, it must be made necessarily in a public deed, and in case of a testamentary act, to observe the prescribed solemnities.

Let us now consider the problem of irregularity that may occur during the life of this contract, because there are specific causes for voiding foreseen in Articles 2779–2780 that make use of the voiding of the contract of rent for life if the person over whose life expectancy it has taken place has already died before the granting. Also the contract is declared void if the pensioner dies into the term that is appointed in it and which will not be less than thirty days, counted from the granting.

As for its form of termination, this contract of life interest must end precisely on the death of the person over whose life it has been constituted, in case that this coincides with the person of the same pensioner, but if the interest was constituted over the life of a third party, then the interest must be transmitted to his or her heirs (i.e., to the pensioner's heirs), until the person over whose provision it was may die.

An irregular form of termination of this contract consists in the possibility that the debtor may have caused the death of the creditor, or else the death of the person over whose life the rent may have been made. Article 2791 states that in this case the capital must be returned to the owner (or to legitimate heirs).

Chapter 4. Acquisition and Administration of the Estate

§1. The Acquisition of the Estate

221. One of the most important rules in succession law adopted in the system of the CCDF – and, in general, in all of the civil codes of the Mexican Republic – consists in the opening of the succession in a retroactive form at the moment when the author of the estate dies (Article 1649).

This constitutes, of course, a legal fiction. In fact, what frequently happens in hereditary facts is that most people let the time pass without doing any further action and this may be due to different causes.

Thus, according to this succession rule, the fact of accepting or disclaiming the estate are claimed to be retroactive effects to the date of testator's death (Article 1660).

That same Article 1649 states as well, as a specific cause of exception, that succession must also be claimed at the precise moment when the assumption of death of an absent person is declared (Article 705).

Matching this with the precept that states the general opening rule of succession, Article 1652 states that the right to claim an estate prescribes in a period of time of ten years. This term is transmitted to the heirs. At what moment does the term start to run? A sentence of the federal tribunals has resolved that:

> In view that no legal precept from the Civil Code or Civil Procedure Code points out at what moment the term for the operation of the prescription of the action of petition of estate will start, it must be understood that this starts to run from the moment when the right may be demandable, and this may not be other than that in which it is put into possession to the demand of the goods belonging to the hereditary mass by means of recognition of its quality of heir by the competent authority; and it is starting at the moment when the term of ten years of the extinctive prescription of the action must start to count.[130]

However, it is necessary to clarify here that, diversely, the right to denounce a succession cannot be limited in time. Thus, a former sentence from the Supreme Court of Justice of the Nation resolved that:

> The right to denounce the successory trial cannot be limited in time and, therefore, the inheriting and accepting the estate, because our Mexican law, following the Roman and the ancient Spanish laws that inspired it, and setting apart on this point of the French one, maintains that tradition and does not contain any precept that may establish such time limitation.[131]

130. Cesáreo Chatú de León [1996] III S.J.F. 321.
131. Felipe R. Hernández [1960] IV S.C.J.N. 252.

222. Now, what is the *procedure to* open the estate? At this point two possibilities are settled: if the succession is of a testamentary nature, and there is an executor, then it falls under the responsibility of this person to claim the inheritance, either in judicial or notarial venue, under penalty of loss of the charge.

The second possibility occurs when there is no executor appointed, either for omission in the respective testamentary disposition, or because it is a succession with a statutory character. If this is so, each one of the heirs may claim the estate.

223. The representative of the succession is called *albacea*. This is a word of Arabic origin that means the person charged by the testator – or by the judge – to fulfil the last will of the deceased. In the procedure of the statutory succession, the executor is directly named by a judge in a meeting that gathers all coheirs and where the designation will be made (Article 805 CPCDF and Articles 1683–1685 CCDF). This meeting is only omitted in cases where the heirs were unique or if the persons interested on the answer to the calling may have given their vote. The executor has the obligation to legally protest the charge.

224. In order to become an executor, the person must have full capacity, have an honest way of living, and not have been condemned for any kind of crime against property. Besides, the Code establishes that the executor must have a free disposition of goods. Besides, this person must not have been removed from such a charge at any prior time (Articles 1679 and 1680).

225. There are several kinds of executors. In the enumeration of the Code, the executor may be universal, special, joint, and general.

The *universal executor* is of a unique character. He must be responsible for the administration and representation of all the hereditary mass. When it is not so, the law says that he is an executor of *special* character, and in this case the charge is exercised according to the order of its designation and according to the values or goods that may be specially consignated to him.

The *joint executor* results from the plural condition of the charge, because in this case the people who may receive such character have to work with other executors in harmony, according to a majority of votes, and in an extreme case, with judicial decision. There is one exception, on cases of extreme urgency, because in this hypothesis anybody may practice the acts that may necessarily result, although of course the obligation to inform the others is always kept intact.

Finally, the executor with 'a general character' denomination is not but a reiterative name that utilizes the Code in Articles 1701 and 1706 for the same case as the universal executor.

226. In case of excuses, Article 1698 prevents that the following people may be excused to be executors: the employees and public functionaries; the militaries; those so poor that they cannot attend to the executor's duty without harming their subsistence; those people with habitual bad health, or illiterate; those who may be 60 years old; and those people with another executor's duty.

Such justification must be presented necessarily within a term no longer than six days following the naming, under penalty of payment of consequential damages and loss of profits.

227. Apart from the institution of the executor, our Code mentions as well other succession representation, we mean the figure of the *intervenor* (Article 1728). The functions of this intervenor are reduced to the surveillance of the executor. Thus, if any heir may not agree with the naming of the executor by the majority, the person has the right to name an intervenor to watch over the executor. An important characteristic of this figure is that the intervenor cannot have, in any case, the possession of goods.

As to the rest, the intervenor must have the capacity that is required in general juridical acts. The intervenor charge results in an indefinite endurance according to the nature of his task, that is, watching over the executor. There are, however, specific cases where the intervention of this representative is typical. This happens when, for example, the heir is absent, or unknown, or when the sum of the legacies is equal to, or larger than, the sum of the heir executor and, finally, when establishments of public assistance are designated for legacies.

228. The executor must be remunerated. Our legislation mentions the payment of 2% over the total of the inheritance, and it even extends it up to 5% in respect of industrial yieldings. However, this situation results only from the absence of expressed retribution on the part of the testator, although the executor has the right to choose between both. The retribution can also be in specie.

229. The executor's functions are complex. The charge contains several obligations that are listed in Article 1706 CCDF, such as the presentation of the testament; the insurance of the goods of the inheritance; the formation of inventories; the administration of the goods and accounts reports; the payment of the mortuary, hereditary, and testamentary debts; the partition and adjudication of goods between the heirs and legataries; the defence, in a trial and out of it, of the succession and the will, and finally, that of representing the succession.

The precept is reiterated with different dispositions dispersed in the rest of the chapter. One of the most important is foreseen in Article 1708 that refers to get guarantee of performing the charge with deposit, mortgage, or pledge, according to the basis stipulated there. In another case, some of the obligations are only complemented with more specific dispositions, as in Articles 1711 and 1706, fr. I, that imposes the presentation of the testament within eight days following the testator's death.

230. Generally, the responsibility of the executor is reduced ineludibly to the payment of consequential damages and loss of profits, in a more specific form (e.g., Articles 1713–1715), or in a general form (Article 1722).

One of the main executor's obligations, that of giving account, is even transmitted to his or her heirs. The executor is also personally responsible for those who may work under his/her orders.

231. The Code prevents a list of fair causes for the termination of the function of executor which, by the way, extends to the labour of the intervenor. These are the natural endings of the charge, death, legal incapacity, legitimate excuses (with attendance of the interested, and the Public Prosecutor, when minors or the System for the Family Integral Development are affected); finishing the term appointed by law; revoking of their naming; and remotion (Article 1745 CCDF).

232. There are specific rules in Mexican law for the acceptance or renounce disclaim of the estate. Articles 1653–1678 deal with the subject.

The acceptance of an estate may be made in only two forms: expressly or tacitly. With this same expression its intrinsic qualities are characterized (Article 1656). However, it is true that the acceptance as well as the renunciation must be made in a plain form and our legislation does not admit partial acceptance or renunciation, or subject to condition or term. Somehow, it is clear that it is in any case about a decision of a personal character that of course does not exclude a collective acceptance or renunciation that is, done by all heirs.

The right to accept or renounce the estate is transmitted to the successors (Article 1659). The under-aged and other disabled, logically, do not have the capacity to accept or disclaim the estate, and they need to complete their personality through the titular institution. But even to effect renunciation, they need judicial authorization along with prior audience from the Public Prosecutor. Our Code still prescribes that the wife does not need the authorization of the husband to accept or reject (Article 1655).

What happens if the heir does not declare his intention to accept or renounce the estate? In this case, anybody with a legitimate interest may request the judge in charge to fix a term for him/her to decide about the fact. In any case, Article 1669 states that in case an answer may not be obtained at all, the estate will be regarded as accepted.

Nevertheless, in case of renunciation there is a specific formality. The general rule is that renunciation must be necessarily made before the judge who deals with the case, whether it is intestate succession or testamentary succession. However, the law asks for an exception: when the heir is not at the place of the trial, the renunciation may be granted eventually by public instrument before a notary public (Article 1661).

233. Besides the acceptation and renounce, a third figure that appears in the case is the simple and general rejection (*repudio*) to the estate. It is true that our Civil Code talks specifically about renunciation (*renuncia*) in Articles 1665 and 1667 too, but there does not seem to be any kind of foundation to believe that it is about two different institutions. However, some part of the doctrine believes that rejection implies only the non-acceptance of the estate, without the designation of a specific person benefited by the act; instead, the act of renunciation would admit the designation of another person to whom the rights are transmitted, with which it would be compared to the figure of cession of hereditary rights that we have already analysed in another part of this monograph (compare paragraph 213).

We have already commented that according to that stated in Article 1291, transactions cannot be made in respect to the inheritance until the death of the author has occurred. This same rule is repeated in Article 1665, specifying that 'Nobody may reject the succession of a living person or alienate the rights that he may have eventually to his estate.' Succession cannot be accepted or rejected without the certainty of the death of the author either.

Logically, moral persons may equally accept or reject estates, except when it is about official institutions or public assistance institutions, because these persons must be submitted to specific dispositions precisely stated in the new Article 1668.

234. The principle established in the CCDF is the irrevocability of the acceptance or rejection. Thus, once the decision has been taken and expressed in the legal form, the act may not be impugned except for reasons of bad faith or violence (Articles 1816 and 1818, respectively).

But what happens if there is a future alteration to the quality or quantity of the estate? In this case, the norm states that the act may be revoked if, under the consequence of an unknown testament at that time, such alteration emerges.

Naturally, it is not allowed that the rejection of the estate may harm creditors and Article 1673 authorizes to request a resolution to accept the estate in the name of the debtor, on the part of the creditors. However, this case presents a peculiar complication. The creditors only have the right to benefit from the estate exclusively in what corresponds to the payment of their credits; therefore, if there is any excess, to whom must it be given? It is clear that it cannot be given to the presumptive heir who has rejected it, even for the bad faith with which this person has been conduced. Therefore, in this case it must be made by calling on the other heirs, according to their legal order. In this last hypothesis, whoever comes to the estate may pay the creditors and then the subrogation in the rights of whoever has verified the rejection is produced (Articles 1676 and 2058 fr. III).

Finally, it is a rule of right that the eventual acceptance of the estate does not produce *confusion* in the goods of the author and his/her heirs, because the CCDF selects up the general principle that the entire estate is understood as accepted under the benefit of a rigorous inventory (Articles 1678 and 2208).

§2. The Administration of the Estate

235. The CCDF (Articles 1295 and 1599) and the CPCDF (Articles 790 and 799) command two different forms of the succession trials, according to the two types of inheritances: testate probate proceeding (by will), or intestate succession proceeding (*ab intestato*).

Nonetheless, there are stated rules that are equally applied to both kinds of succession. Thus, we have already seen that our law expressly defines the concept of inheritance in both cases, stating that 'Estate is the succession in all of the goods of the deceased and in all of his rights and duties that may not be extinguished by death' (Article 1281). It is also as a disposition of common application, that the heir acquires under *universal* title. Therefore, he or she responds to all the hereditary obligations which the goods may cover; meanwhile, the legatary acquires under *particular* title and therefore, he/she does not have any more obligations than those which are expressly imposed by the testator.

In some cases, however, the testator may not have stipulated the transmission of all goods. In these cases, this irregular situation in the provision of the author must be changed for the legal normative: thus, a part of the inheritance – that which was expressed – will be ruled by the norms concerning the will dispositions and the testamentary succession; the remaining part – that is, the one omitted – will be ruled by the legal articles corresponding to the statutory succession.

236. We have already expressed that Articles 1649 and 1660 claim the retroactivity of the effects of the succession precisely at the moment of decedent's death. In consonance with this disposition, the CPCDF states that once the death of a person occurs, the necessary providences to ensure the goods will be immediately dictated. These urgent measures for maintaining of goods are gathering the document of the deceased, which closed and sealed, will be deposited in the secret of the Court; ordering the mail service to remit the mailing that might come for the author of the succession, with which he will do the same as with all of the other documents, and to send the money and jewels, or some other goods, to be deposited in the establishment authorized by law (Article 770).

The Public Prosecutor will attend to the proceeding of insurance of goods. However, such a ministerial intervention is infrequent. Commonly the relatives of the interested party present the respective documents to start, in this case, the succession trial in whichever of both modalities. Certainly, Article 774 of the CPCDF demands the presentation of the death certificate of the author of the estate – or any other sufficient document or proof.

237. In the case of *testate probate proceeding*, along with the death certificate of the author of the inheritance, the will must be presented as well. Article 790 CPCDF says in the same initial act, the judge must call the concerned persons to a meeting for designation of an executor. The law imposes peremptory terms to the judicial authority. Unfortunately, because of the excessive amount of cases before the tribunals, these terms can hardly be accomplished.

Once verified, and unless there is any refutation or objection of the incapability of the interested parties, the judge must then recognize them as heirs under will terms.

238. The procedure is slightly different in the case of the *intestate succession proceeding*. Anyhow, in this case the document of burial must be presented, according to that stated for both hypotheses in Article 774 CPCDF. Along with this indispensable document, the petitioner must present as well the document that may prove the family relationship with the author of the estate (or else, the document that may prove any other kind of pertinent relationship). But besides that, in the own writing of accusation, the presumptive heir is obliged to refer the names and domiciles of all of the other relatives in a straight line, if there were any, and of the collaterals up to the fourth degree, in case of absence of the first ones. The name and the address of the widow or widower must also be mentioned. Based on these terms, the judge will open the succession and must proceed to notify all of the interested parties for them to request their hereditary rights.

Once all gathered in public audience, the legal intervention will be given to the Public Prosecutor, who will formulate a 'pediment' in the terms that it may proceed, watching at all times the legally corresponding norms and in any case the public interest, if there were any. In this same audience, the interested parties must surrender testimonial information in the sense that they are the sole heirs of the deceased. The process is so expeditious that once the prior proceedings have been completed, the judge must dictate a declarative resolution of heirs without hesitation, in the terms foreseen by law.

There is even a more expeditious procedure in notarial or judicial venue, according to Article 815*bis* through 815*sextus*. It is denominated a 'especial procedure', because it has place in just a meeting, if there is not controversy among the presumptive heirs and all of them are of age. By a legal fiction, these declarations substitute the assumed will of the author of the estate.

Quite often, in this same resolution the appointment of executor is made, if the heirs were unique or the interested parties, from their initial promotion, may have given their vote in a written form or in a personal attendance. If this were not the case, then the judge must call for another meeting of heirs within the peremptory term of eight days and it is then that an executor is designated. This executor has a definite character, as it is foreseen by Article 805 CPCDF.

There are special circumstances, though, that may occur. This is, for example, when the declaration of heirs is requested only by collateral relatives inside the fourth degree, because then the judge must publish edicts announcing the death without testament and the names of the claimers, calling any other interested parties. Then the procedure retakes again its normal flow in the terms foreseen by the prior articles.

It may happen as well that remote relatives may present themselves as a consequence of notice by publication. In this case, the petitioners must justify their family relationship accompanying even a genealogical tree which may show graphically the nearest *parentala* with the decedent.

Even in any of these situations of exception, the procedure necessarily ends up, no matter how, in the declarative resolution of heirs foreseen in Article 803. This declaration of heirs is equivalent to a title of legitimate possession of goods, rights and actions of the deceased, in the terms foreseen by the diverse Article 812 CPCDF. Once this is completed, the executor must receive all of the goods that conform the common property of the succession.

239. We have already made a reference at another different point (paragraphs 223 et seq.) to the different forms or successory representation. Well then, the definite executor, designated precisely in the terms foreseen in Article 805 CPCDF, has as an immediate obligation, the formation of the inventory. There are certain specific rules for this. Thus, the CPCDF prescribes that the executor has ten days to proceed, and it disposes that within a term of sixty days he must conclude the inventory, under penalty of remotion of charge.

The inventory may be done in the judicial venue, as well as in the notarial one. In both cases, it must be proceeded to appoint all the interested parties. Article 820 says that the notary public or the executor will proceed, on the appointed meeting day, to make the description of goods with all clarity and precision in the following order: money, jewels, commerce or industry, legal documents, livestock, fruits, furniture, real estate, credits, documents and important papers in general, and even someone else's goods that the deceased may have had in his power in *comodato*, deposit, pledge or under any other title.

Next, the designated expert – either by majority of votes or by judicial agreement – must proceed to value all of the goods inventoried according to the described procedure. Once this is completed, the inventory must be added to the case and they will be put under disposition of the concerned parties within a term of five working days; the judge must then approve them without any reserves, except in case of manifest opposition, in whose hypothesis it must be proceeded to decide the question.

It is a general rule, stated in Article 829 CPCDF, that the inventory made by the executor or by any of the heirs, takes advantage, but it does not harm, all of the other interested parties.

It is interesting to note, finally, that this obligation of the executor is found sanctioned in case of unaccomplishment with the loss or remotion of the charge, dictated plainly –*de plano*, that is, without invoking any article for it.

240. It has been previously said that the designation of heirs turns the beneficiary automatically into the legitimate owner of the goods. Thus it has been defined, certainly, in a sentence of 1995 stating that:

> The right to possession of hereditary goods, is legally transmitted to heirs and to universal executors, from the moment of death of the author of the estate, just the way it is stated by Article 1704 of the Civil Code, for which even when the petitioner may not be considered to have a property title, properly said, because this one remains defined with the adjudication that may be verified in the respective successory trial, in any way, by inheriting due to the death of the author of succession, and by being declared universal heir of that by the legitimate trial, he is no longer found in a mere expectative of right, but he also acquires the right to juridical possession of hereditary goods.[132]

However, we should clarify that when a *supérstite* spouse attends to the succession, this one will have, by expressed disposition of Article 832, the possession and administration of the goods of the marital society with intervention of the designated executor. This executor reduces exclusively his/her function to the protection of the administration of the spouse.

241. We have already examined as well in another place (compare paragraph 227) the actuation of the intervenor as the representative of the succession. Our CCDF regulates the functions of this intervenor in Articles 1728 et seq. Now we must add that another one of the specific activities of the intervenor consists in promoting the necessary lawsuits to defend the goods that constitute the common property of the estate, either in an active form, or in a passive form. However, this

132. Natividad and Gerardo Hernández Barrios and Sofía Barrios Lara [1995] II S.J.F. 490.

hypothesis may only be updated when once the succession trial has started and has passed a month's time, there may not be an executor for any reason.

242. The CCDF is very clear in the sense that, during all the time of preparation of the succession trial, the goods that may have been enlisted must not be alienated. This is the general rule. There are only a few cases of exception. They refer to the maintenance and administration of the estate, to repair costs, to hard and expensive maintenance, and to the rise of advantageous conditions for the alienation of goods (Article 841 CPCDF).

Out of all of these cases, it is clear that the inventoried goods must not be alienated. The legal context of this generical prohibition and the admitted cases of exception are found in Articles 1717 and 1758 of the CCDF, and 841 of the CPCDF.

243. One of the main obligations of the representatives of the succession, either intervenor, executor (provisional, judicial or definite), or even the *supérstite* spouse in the case that we have already examined (*supra*, paragraph 176), is the one of *surrendering accounts*. The presentation of accounts has a yearly periodicity and it includes the deposit of the fruits in terms of that ordered in Article 846 CPCDF. These accounts must be published by the court secretary for their examination of interested parties within a maximum of ten days. In case of opposition, the respective incident must be followed (Article 852 CPCDF).

Out of this periodical delivery of accounts, the final obligation of the executor is solved in the surrendering of general accounts, once paying off is concluded. This final account must as well be submitted to examination by the interested parties and it is then susceptible to refutation.

244. Paying off means, in the proper terms of the Civil Code, any debt whose amount may have been determined or may be determined within nine days (Article 2189 CCDF). Under these conditions, and once made the inventory, the executor must proceed to pay off the estate. To such effect, Articles 1754–1766 of the same CCDF indicate in a prioritized form, which are the debts that must be paid, precisely as follows: mortuary debts; expenses (or rigorous maintenance and administration of the estate); food credits; food debts; and legacy payments.

Along with this obligation of expenses, the CPCDF states at the same time the obligation of distributing at least in a provisional form, the products, either in cash or in specie. The executor must formalize a project and this will be available to the interested parties within five days. The lack of presentation of the project is a cause of automatic separation, according to Article 858, incise 3rd, CPCDF.

245. Once approved the account of general administration, the executor must proceed to *partition of goods*. In this case, three important general principles must be followed. These are:

- the principle of non-indivisibility;
- the principle of partition according to the author's will; and
- the principle of autonomy of will to celebrate the pacts that the coheirs may consider convenient.

The first general principle is found established in Article 1768 that mentions: 'No coheir may oblige himself to remain in the indivisibility of goods, not even by an expressed prevention of the testator.'

The second general principle is found in Article 1771. In the terms of this disposition, the partition of the goods that the author of the estate has arranged, precisely in its terms must be respected (compare Article 863 CPCDF). However, what happens if it was not foreset in such a sense? Then the Code decides, with a great deal of a practical sense, that the professional occupation of every one of the heirs will be attended, in order to obtain the best administration of goods. This takes place particularly in the case where goods may constitute an agriculture, industrial, or commercial, enterprise. In this case, the heirs who may be set aside by the company must receive in cash the part that may correspond to them, according to the value fixed by experts.

Finally, the third general principle, that is, the principle of autonomy of will that must preside in the businesses in civil law, is found established in Article 1772 CCDF that allows, in its final part, that in any case it must be attended to the agreements that may be celebrated among the coheirs. This principle is reinforced by Article 862 CPCDF. But if no agreement is reached, the executor must then be subjected to the legal normative.

Who has the right to request the partition of the estate? According to Article 859 CPCDF, those who have this right are the heir who may have the free disposition of goods; the heirs under condition, as soon as accomplished this one; the cessionary and the creditor of the heir; the coheirs of the conditional heir; and the heirs of the heir who dies before partition.

In the terms of Article 861 CPCDF, the executor must proceed to present the project of partition in twenty-five days, under the penalty of separation of the charge, including of loss of the honoraries, and a cash fine.

Once written, the project of partition will be put to the concerned parties within ten days. Then the procedure of routine is followed for its immediate approval, if an objection may not be formulate –or substantiation of the procedure in case of opposition.

246. The partition adjudicates a proportional part of the goods to each one of the heirs. In this case, Article 1779 CCDF consignates that the partition legally done, fixes the portion of hereditary goods that corresponds to everyone of the heirs.

However, it is convenient to mention some specific rules. For example, in case of loss of the hereditary wages, because in this hypothesis an obligation of indemnization to charges of the other heirs is created, precisely in proportion to their hereditary rights; as is logical, the total amount of the common property must be reduced and according to this new quantity, then, make a new partition.

It may also happen that by adjudicating a credit, it becomes uncashable, in which case the coheirs do not respond the latter insolvency. However, they are responsible for the solvency at the time of the partition (Article 1785 CCDF). Naturally, if the credit is of itself unrecoverable, no responsibility is established at all.

247. The epigraph 'On rescission and voiding of partitions' conforms to the last chapter that is found in the Civil Code in respect to successory partitions. The general established rule remits the causes of irregularity precisely as set out in Articles 2224–2242, that regulate the cases of generic voidness, that is, for all kind of obligations.

A specific case of voidness has its origin in the excluded heir (Articles 1375 and 1789 CCDF). The excluded heir is the one who, for some reason, has been replaced in his or her hereditary rights and then petitions for a new partition, which will include the part that should have been given to him/her.

So, what happens in the case of a false heir? If this happens, the law expressly says that the effected partition is void, but only as to the relationship with the impostor, in honour of the principle *utile per inutile non vitiatur* that we have already mentioned (see Article 2238 CCDF). In this case, the part unduly applicated returns then as a surplus to the other coheirs.

Let us now suppose, finally, that once the partition is effected, other problems may arise. A partition of a supplementary character may be made, then, but Article 1791 CCDF demands again the observance of all the legal requirements. Certainly, the diverse Article 829 CPCDF mentions that 'Approved the inventory by the judge or with the consent of all of the interested parties, it cannot be reformed, except by mistake or bad faith declared by definite sentence, pronounced in an ordinary trial.'

248. Logically, the partition must consist of a public document before a notary when it is about goods that must be ruled by that formality (Article 1777). If it is referring to personal property goods or any other kind of rights that may not be set in a public instrument, the formality is reduced then to the celebration of a private agreement among the interested parties (compare Article 868 CPCDF). Article 869 of the same code states in detail the requirements that the respective instrument of partition must contain. It is as follows: the names, measures and boundaries of the lots adjudicated, with expression of the part that every adjudicatory heir may have the obligation to give back, if the price of the house exceeds that of his portion or to receive in case it is missing; the special warranty due to the possible devolution of the excess; the enumeration of the furniture or shared amounts; notice of the delivery of the titles of adjudicated properties; amounts that some heir remains recognizing another, and respective warranty; and the signature of all interested.

249. It remains to consider here, finally, the important participation that the Mexican law grants in all these cases to the intervention of the notaries public (compare Articles 1776 CCDF and 817, 820 and 872–876*bis* CPCDF). We have already said that those interested parties in the succession may now choose any of two procedures for its resolution, that is, the judicial venue or the notarial venue. Well then, the intervention of the notary confers much more speed to the procedure without excessive cost to the interested party. For such effect, certain conditions must be gathered, specifically that all the heirs must be of age, that the interest of the tax office – if there were any – be covered, and that, in its case, the minors may have been duly represented. Article 872 CPCDF adds the requirement that there may not be any controversy.

In the particular of testamentary procedure, the interested parties must be present before the notary exhibiting the deceased party of the author of the estate and the respective will. The interested parties, however, must write down an instrument in which everybody accepts the estate, recognizes among themselves their hereditary rights and declares that the executor will proceed to form an inventory of the goods that may constitute the hereditary mass.

Once this is done, the notary will order the publishing of edicts to give publicity to the act. Once the inventory has been completed by the executor and all people being in agreement, the notary must proceed to *protocolización*, that is to say, the act becoming a public document. The same thing happens with the project of partition, once it has been formulated.

By other hand, in the case of intestate succession, Article 876 CPCDF demands as well the same requirements of being of age and agreement of the interested parties. However, the demand of the presentation of the judicial resolution of heirs is added. The judge must inquire the interested parties to designate the respective notary public.[133]

Logically, when there is an opposition from a presumptive heir, or even from a third person, or a creditor, the notary is obliged to suspend his/her intervention.

Finally, in correspondence with the reformation that we have already commented on about the public simplified testament (compare paragraph 195), the respective provincial civil procedures codes states the specific procedure applicable to the notarial intervention in these cases.

133. The CC of the State of Puebla (Art. 3526) even authorizes the interested parties to request the sending of the case to a notary public and to adopt the necessary agreements for ending the procedure.

Selected Bibliography

§1. Books

Acosta, R.M., et al. *Código Civil para el Distrito Federal. Comentarios, legislación, doctrina y jurisprudencia*. Vols I–V. Mexico: Porrúa, 1998.

Arce y, C.J. *De las sucesiones*. 5th edn. Mexico: Porrúa, 1998.

Aspe, A.V. *Familia. Naturaleza, derechos y responsabilidades*. Mexico: Porrúa, 2006.

Baqueiro, R.E. & B.R. Buenrostro. *Derecho de familia y sucesiones*. Mexico: Harla, 1990.

Begné, P. *La mujer en Mexico. Su situación legal*. Mexico: Trillas, 1998.

Castañeda, R.M.L. *El Derecho civil en México. Dos siglos de historia*. México: Porrúa, 2013.

Chávez, A.M.F. *La familia en el derecho*. Vols I–IV. Mexico: Porrúa, 1996–1999.

Chávez, A.M.F. *La familia en el derecho. Relaciones jurídicas conyugales*. Mexico: Porrúa, 2007.

Domínguez, M.J.A. *Derecho civil. Parte general. Personas. Cosas. Negocio jurídico e invalidez*. 6th edn. Mexico: Porrúa, 1998.

Domínguez, M.J.A. *Derecho de familia*. Mexico: Porrúa, 2011.

Domínguez, M.J.A. *Derecho civil. Sucesiones*. Mexico: Porrúa, 2013.

Galindo, G.I. *Derecho civil. Primer curso. Parte general. Personas. Familia*. 17th edn. Mexico: Porrúa, 1998.

Galván, R.F. *El concubinato en el vigente derecho mexicano*. México: Porrúa, 2013.

Gómez, F.C. *Derecho Procesal Familiar*. México: Porrúa, 2013.

Gutiérrez y, G.E. *Derecho sucesorio. Inter vivos y mortis causa*. 2nd edn. Mexico: Porrúa, 1997.

Gutiérrez y, G.E. *Derecho civil para la familia*. Mexico: Porrúa, 2011.

Herrerías, S.M.M. *El concubinato. Análisis histórico jurídico y su problemática en la práctica*. Mexico: Porrúa, 1998.

Ibarrola de, A. *Cosas y sucesiones*. 8th edn. Mexico: Porrúa, 1998.

Ibarrola de, A. *Derecho de familia*. 4th edn. Mexico: Porrúa, 1993.

Instituto de Investigaciones Jurídicas (ed.). *Diccionario Jurídico Mexicano*. 13th edn. Vols I–IV. Mexico: Porrúa, 1999.

Instituto de Investigaciones Jurídicas (ed.). *Código Civil para el Distrito Federal en Materia Común y para toda la República en Materia Federal, Comentado*. 5th edn. Vols I–VI. Mexico: Miguel Angel Porrúa, 1998.

Magallón, I.J.M. *Instituciones de derecho civil*. Vols I–VII. Mexico: Porrúa, 1990–1998.

Martínez, A.S.T. *El régimen patrimonial del matrimonio en Mexico*. 3rd edn. Mexico: Porrúa, 1991.
Olivera T., J. *El daño moral*. 1st edn. Mexico: Themis, 1993.
Pérez Duarte y, N.A.E. *La obligación alimentaria. Deber jurídico, deber moral*. 2nd edn. Mexico: Porrúa, 1998.
Pina de, R. *Elementos de derecho civil mexicano*. Vols I–V. Mexico: Porrúa, 1993–1999.
Rico, A.F., G.P. Bandala & C.M. Cohen. *Derecho de familia*. México: Porrúa, 2011.
Rendón, U.C.E. *La Tutela*. México: Porrúa, 2001.
Rojina, V.R. *Derecho civil mexicano*. Vols I–VI. Mexico: Porrúa, 1997–1999.
Ruíz, L.R. *Jurisprudencia familiar 1917–1998*. Mexico: Porrúa, 1998.
Sánchez, M.R. *Derecho civil. Parte general. Personas y familia*. Mexico: Porrúa, 1998.
Sánchez, M.R. *Los grandes cambios en el derecho de familia de Mexico*. 20th edn. Mexico: Porrúa, 1991.
Tapia, R.J. *Derecho de Familia*. México: Porrúa, 2012.
Vargas, D.L.D. *Aspectos prácticos del contrato de fideicomiso*. México: Porrúa, 2012.
Zavala, P.D.H. *Derecho familiar*. Mexico: Porrúa, 2008.
Zamora, S., et al. *Mexican Law*. New York: Oxford University Press, 2004.

§2. ARTICLES

Arce y, C.J. 'La libre testamentificación en el código civil y sus antecedentes históricos'. R.D.C. 1 (September 1998): 41.
Barrera, Z.F. 'Hacia una mejor normatividad jurídica del concubinato en el Código Civil del Distrito Federal'. R.F.D.M. XLV, 203–204 (September–December 1995): 161.
Brena, S.I. 'Testamento público simplificado, sus posibles consecuencias'. R.D.P. 16 (January–April 1995): 17.
Casillas, C.C. 'Los bienes matrimoniales en las legislaciones estatales'. R.D.N. 101 (June 1990): 57.
Cruz, P.L. 'Situación patrimonial del cónyuge menor de edad (comentarios a los artículos 641, 643 y 173 del Código Civil del Distrito Federal)'. R.D.P. 16 (January–April 1995): 139.
Flores, E. 'Naturaleza jurídica de los derechos de la personalidad'. R.F.D.M. XLVIII, no. 221–222 (September–December 1998): 39.
Galindo, G.I. 'La filiación y la paternidad'. R.F.D.M. XXVIII, no. 110 (May–August 1978): 395.
García, R.S. 'Reformas en materia civil y familiar'. R.M.J. II, no. 4 (October–December 1984): 393.
Gómez-Robledo, V.A. 'Mexico consagra la doble nacionalidad'. R.D.P. no. 23 (May–August 1997): 131.
Lagunes, P.I. 'La tutela dativa popular'. R.F.D.M. XLIV, nos 195–196 (May–August 1994): 149.

Luna, T.R. 'Los regímenes matrimoniales en las legislaciones de los estados de la república'. R.D.N. 104 (October 1993): 3.
Magallón, I.J.M. 'El perfil social del patrimonio de familia'. R.F.D.M. XLVII, no. 211–212 (January–April 1997): 247.
Moncayo, R.S. 'Consideraciones en torno al matrimonio entre los aztecas'. E.J. 4 (1997): 89.
Morineau, M. 'El parentesco según una sentencia del Tercer Tribunal Colegiado en Materia Civil'. R.D.P. 21 (September–December 1996): 139.
Núñez, B.P. 'Sucesión universal o sucesiones'. R.D.P. 13–15 (January–December 1994): 93.
Pacheco, E.A. 'El llamado testamento biológico (*Living will*)'. R.D.N. 111 (April 1998): 251.
Pérez, C.M.M. 'Violencia intrafamiliar'. R.F.D.M. XLVIII, nos 219–220 (May–August 1998): 67.
Pérez F. del, C.B. 'La adopción'. R.D.N. 113 (July 1999): 91.
Rodríguez, M.E. 'La adopción de menores y las recientes reformas del 28 de mayo de 1998 a los códigos civil y de procedimientos civiles del Distrito Federal'. R.D.C. 1 (September 1998): 207.
Siqueiros, J.L. 'La atribución y la pérdida de la nacionalidad mexicana'. R.D.P. 17 (May–August 1995): 211.
Zubiría, M.E. 'Regímenes sucesorios en los Estados Unidos Mexicanos'. R.M.D. 1 (May 1999): 17.

Selected Bibliography

Index

The numbers here refer to paragraph numbers. The letter n following the paragraph number, designates a note.

Absentees
  generalities, 20
  right of the, 163
  and succession, 161
Accounts
  approval of, 244
  paying of, 243
  surrendering of, 242
Acquisition of the Estate
  generalities, 229
  procedure, 230
Adoption
  certificates of, 26
  international, 101, 107
  procedure, 103
  requirements, 101
  revoke, 105
  simple, 104
  succession in case of, 177, 190
  total (or plain), 104, 106
Adultery
  as cause of divorce, 78
  as cause of revoke of marital donations, 150
  as impediment to celebrate marriage, 63
  as incapacity to inherit, 170
Aliens
  activities and rights, 169
  adoption from, 101, 107
  guardianship, 122
  incapacity to inherit, 172
  limited of capacity, 168
  marriage, 72
Alimony
  concept, 68
  in concubinage, 85
  principles, 69
Artificial insemination
  as cause of divorce, 78
  and legal maternity, 85, *n.* 3
Assets, 79, 83

Bona vacantia, 191

Capacity
  of enjoyment, 16
  of exercise, 16
  to make a will, 194
  to marry, 62
  of moral person, 17
  to succeed, 164, 167
Certificates (of Civil Registry)
  of adoption, 26
  of birth, 24
  of corrections, 33
  of emancipation, 28
  forms of the, 23
  of guardianship, 27
  of inscription of statements, 32
  of marriage, 29, 66
  of recognition, 25
Children
  abuse, *see* Punishment
  birth of, 86
  born in wedlock, 86
  born out of wedlock, 92
contracts with, 112, 114, 131
  education, 112
  incapacity, 18
  rights of the, 6, 18, *n.* 1, 68, 111, *n.* 1
Citizenship
  and adoption, *see* Adoption (international)
  and capacity, 16
Civil Registry, 22
Concubinage
  adoption in, 101
  and alimony, 85, *n.* 2
  concept of, 85, *n.* 1

consequences, 85
generalities, 84
right to inherit, 180
Curatela, 135
Custody, 82, 96, 109, *n.* 1, 110

Death
assumed, 21, 162
certificate of, 31
of the testator, 160
Divorce
causes of, 78
certificate of, 30
effects, 81–83
grounds, 74
procedure, 76–80
types of, 76–78
Domicile
and divorce, 78
elements of, 54, *n.* 1
generalities, 54
and marriage, 67, 148
of moral people, 55
and neighbourhood, 56
and residence, 55
Donations
between spouses, 149
in general, 223
pre-marital, 150

Emancipation, 28
Estate
acceptance of the, 231
acts *inter vivos*, 221
administration of the, 238, 241
and donations, 223
rejection of the, 231
resignation of the, 232
Executor
capacity of the, 182
excuses, 184
fees, 186
generalities, 181
kinds of, 183
obligations, 187
responsibility, 188
termination of the charge, 189

Family
codes of, 8
courts of, 13
importance of law of the, 80
Family violence
as cause of divorce, 78, *n.* 1
as impediment to celebrate marriage, 63
laws on, 111
and parental authority, 117
Fideicomiso
generalities, 224
limitations, 226
nature, 225
termination, 226
Fidelity (duty of), 67, *n.* 1
Filiation, 85, *n.* 3, 86–90
Funeral expenses, *see* Mortuary debts

Guardianship
certificates of, 27
dative, 126
excuses, 128
generalities, 120
kinds of, 123
legitimate, 125
nature, 121, *n.* 1
obligations, 130
termination, 134
testamentary, 124
warranties, 129

Heir
classes, 175
false, 246
presumptive, 161
Housing (right to the), 6, 67

Incapacity, *see* Interdiction
Incest, 24
Inheritance
ascendants, 178
in case of crime, 170
classes, 175
legitimate inheritance, 160
Insurance, 227
Interdiction
causes of, 18
concept of, 19
as condition for guardianship, 121
incapable husband, 89
legal incapacity, 19
mentally handicapped persons, 57–59
natural incapacity, 19
procedure to declare the, 58
Intestate, 160, 237

Kinship
  affinity, 139
  by blood, 138
  civil, 140
  concept of, 137, *n.* 1
  and concubinage, 139, *n.* 1
  as impediment to celebrate marriage, 63
  kinds, 137
  rights to inherit, 175

Legitimacy, 100

Marital society, 152–155
Marriage
  capacity, 62
  certificate of, 29, 66
  concept, 61
  effects, 67
  formalities, 64
  impediments, 63, 65
  nature, 60
  outside, 66
  principles, 142–146
  voidables, 71
  voids, 71
Marriage settlements, 150
Matrimonial home, 67, 148
Mexican United States
  Civil provincial codes, expedition dates, 7, *n.* 1
  Family Law in, 2–4, 8
  population of, 1
  Succession Law in, 2–4
Mortuary debts, 187, 241, 243

Name
  change of the, 47–49
  composition, 36–39
  first, 50
  generalities, 35
  right to the, 34
Nasciturus, 14, 16, 164
Nationality, 51–53
Neighbourhood, 56
Notaries
  intervention in successions, 247–248
  law of the, 93
  and parental authority, 110
  responsibility of, 202
  transactions between spouses, 149
  wills, intervention in, 199–203, 231

Parental Authority
  concept of, 108
  consent to marry, 62–63
  excuses, 119
  limitations, 118
  loss, 117
  suspension, 116
  termination, 115
Partition
  consequences, 245
  formality of the, 247
  principles of the, 244
  rescission of the, 246
  right to request, 244
  voidness of the, 246
Paternity
  certificates of, 24
  imputation of, 98
  investigation of, 99
  refutation of, 91
Person
  capacity, 16
  definition, 14
  moral, 15, 49, 55
  physical, 15
Personality rights, 34
Pregnancy
  knew about of, 87
  legitimacy of son in, 100
Previous death, 165
Prostitution (as cause of divorce), 78
Punishment, 111, *n.* 1

Rape, 98
Recognition, *see* Certificates of
Residence, 55

Separation of goods, 156–158
Sex (change of), 23, *n.* 1, 78
Simultaneous death, 165
Succeed
  capacity, 164
  unworthiness to succeed, 166
Successions
  acceptance, 231
  concubines, 180
  intestate, 160
  opening, 160
  partition of the, *see* Partition

procedure, 237
rejection, 231
representation of the, 181
resignation, 232
rights of the state, *see Bona vacantia*
testamentary, 192
Surname
acquisition of, 43–46
change of, 47

Testamentary, 192, 236
Trusts, *see Fideicomiso*

Violence, *see* Family violence
Void marriage, 71–73
Voidable marriage, 71–73

Will
cause in a, 220
closed, 200
holograph (or autograph), 204
interpretation, 219
joint will, 209
loss of a, 193
made in a foreign country, 208
maritime, 207
military, 206
private, 205
public, 199
restrictions, 214
revocation of a, 210
simplified, 203
types of, 196

www.ingramcontent.com/pod-product-compliance
Lightning Source LLC
LaVergne TN
LVHW021111300926
849160LV00009B/682
* 9 7 8 9 0 4 1 1 5 8 8 6 4 *